Celtic Druidry

"*Celtic Druidry* is a unique Druid path through the practices and perspectives of Celtic Reconstructivism. For people who are interested in bridging ancient Celtic traditions with modern Druid practice, *Celtic Druidry* is a great resource that provides thorough coverage of the ancient Druid lifestyles, deities, festivals, magic, and divination. It also offers the modern Druid an accessible set of practices to apply to their ongoing path."

DANA O'DRISCOLL, GRAND ARCHDRUID OF THE
ANCIENT ORDER OF DRUIDS IN AMERICA
AND AUTHOR OF *SACRED ACTIONS*

"The trees are singing, animals are speaking, the land is calling—magic is afoot. A wise, skilled, and generous Druidess, a teacher of old ways for a modern world, gifts us with a valuable book of blessings and enchantments to help you remember where you are and why you are here. May the path home open before you."

PHYLLIS CUROTT, WITCH, WICCAN PRIESTESS,
AND AUTHOR OF THE *WITCHES' WISDOM TAROT*

"Trying to explain Druidry is a daunting task as there are several explanations and interpretations available. There is also a lot of debate about how 'Druid' should be spelled too. Through this book, Ellen has expertly taken on explaining Druidry through her personal lens of experience and understanding in a very easy to read and very easy follow approach. Much of Ellen's book is anticipating questions and answering them. I like that. By the end—before the end—of reading this book, the reader is bound to become enthusiastic to learn more about Druidism and even become an apprentice through following their own newly enlightened questions. Thank you, Ellen, for making this available."

JOHN WILLMOTT, HOST OF *NATURE ECHOES*

"Modern Druidry (or Druidism) is fraught with mistakes and pitfalls of false information and practices that have little or nothing to do with ancient Druids. This book goes a long way toward addressing some of the modern misconceptions and pointing the reader in the right direction. While it is pan-Celtic, for want of a better term, it draws heavily on Irish native traditions, which have often been ignored in the past. This is a worthwhile and practical introduction for the beginner or for those who have not developed a sound foundation from which to expand."

LUKE EASTWOOD, AUTHOR OF
THE DRUID'S PRIMER, A PATH THROUGH THE FOREST
AND *THE DRUID GARDEN*

"*Celtic Druidry* is compelling and fulfilling in bringing alive the Druid ways of listening to the spirits of nature and the spirits of the Goddesses and Gods to bring healing and health to the Celtic people. Ellen's book beautifully introduces the ways of the Druids for newbies on their beginning journey. The many incantations for meditation, for the spells the Druids call upon in their practices, are a tremendous source for learning the Druid ways."

NICHOLAS E. BRINK, PH.D., AUTHOR OF
THE POWER OF ECSTATIC TRANCE, BALDR'S MAGIC
AND *BEOWULF'S ECSTATIC TRANCE MAGIC*

Celtic Druidry

RITUALS, TECHNIQUES, & MAGICAL PRACTICES

Ellen Evert Hopman

Destiny Books
Rochester, Vermont

Destiny Books
One Park Street
Rochester, Vermont 05767
www.DestinyBooks.com

Text stock is SFI certified

Destiny Books is a division of Inner Traditions International

Note to the reader: *This book is intended to be an informational guide. The
remedies, approaches, and techniques described herein are meant to supplement, and
not to be a substitute for, professional medical care or treatment. They should not be
used to treat a serious ailment without prior consultation with a qualified health care
professional.*

Cataloging-in-Publication Data for this title is available from the Library of Congress

ISBN 978-1-64411-860-3 (print)
ISBN 978-1-64411-861-0 (ebook)

Printed and bound in the United States by Lake Book Manufacturing, LLC.

The text stock is SFI certified. The Sustainable Forestry Initiative® program
promotes sustainable forest management.

10 9 8 7 6 5 4 3 2 1

Text design and layout by Priscilla Harris Baker
This book was typeset in Garamond Premier Pro with Carphe, Gill Sans, and
Raleway used as display typefaces

To send correspondence to the author of this book, mail a first-class letter to the
author c/o Inner Traditions • Bear & Company, One Park Street, Rochester, VT
05767, and we will forward the communication, or contact the author directly at
elleneverthopman.com.

Scan the QR code and save 25% at InnerTraditions.com.
Browse over 2,000 titles on spirituality, the occult, ancient
mysteries, new science, holistic health, and natural medicine.

Contents

PART I
An Introduction to Druidry
Ancient Wisdom and Modern Knowing

PART 2

Becoming a Druid

How to Practice Druidic Arts, Magic, and Spirituality

PART 3

Druids and Nature

Words of Wisdom from Fellow Druids

Foreword

By Kenneth Proefrock, NMD

It is with great honor that I write this endorsement of Ellen Evert Hopman's most recent work. I have known Ellen since 1998, when Philip Carr-Gomm, then head of the Order of Bards, Ovates, and Druids, introduced us over static-filled dial-up internet connections. I had recently graduated from medical school, finished a residency, and was invited back to my alma mater to teach nutritional biochemistry and botanical medicine. While researching modern interpretations of ancient uses of botanical medicines, I became more interested in how spiritually oriented groups might incorporate historically relevant plant materials into their work, hoping to illustrate how the uses of different botanical medicines have changed and shifted over the centuries. I was looking for modern groups of people who still used botanical medicine as a primary part of their daily lives and might draw from a historical precedent.

Ellen was a clinically trained herbalist who had studied with William LeSassier. In addition to writting several books and articles on botanical medicine, she also ran the Yahoo! discussion group for the Celtic Reconstructionist–based Order of the White Oak, a group whose stated goal was to, as well as could be determined given the archaeological evidence, create a spiritual organization based on the principles and practices of the ancient Celts.

White Oak's expressly stated tripartite mission consisted of: discussion of the lessons of ancient and recent history with peers; studying the Brehon Laws of Ireland, the Celtic Mythological Cycles, the Wisdom Texts, and other ancient sources; and seeking ways to apply this information to contemporary Druidic practice.

The Order's membership, from the beginning, was full of brilliant, strong-willed, independent thinkers who created something spectacular out of a union that was often contentious, always passionate, and often profoundly thought-provoking. The training required actual spiritual cultivation of the membership—one can make conjectures about historical spiritual practice, but one has to experience it firsthand to really "get it." This combination of daily spiritual practice contextualized in a historical structure was personally appealing to me, and Ellen agreed to foster me in the traditions of the Order, most of which you will find in this book. I finished that fostership in 2008, was initiated into the Council of Elders, and later became the sitting president of the Order of the White Oak. The Order's membership has changed drastically over the past twenty-five years, which seems inevitable in some spiritual organizations; those changes represented structural changes in the organization, platform changes in content distribution, and changes in the organization's constituency.

Yahoo! discussion groups are no longer the online meeting place; those have now been replaced with other social media platforms, like Facebook. We are all members of an international community, and virtual friendships with people we have never physically met prevail more than ever. This greater worldwide connection has seemingly left less time and inclination for small groups of like-minded individuals to gather regularly within their local communities. The social media sphere is becoming the conduit through which entertainment and spiritual epiphany are expected to flow. There is also a growing apathy in the population of people involved in social media-driven online spiritual groups. As a group's membership increases, individual participation seems to decrease, expertise can be gleaned from scrolling through prior postings, and the real work of cultivating cognitive literacy is too easily overlooked.

What Ellen is offering you here in this book, is an opportunity to see what some of the most inspiring minds in Celtic Reconstruction created when they came together for a magical time at the turn of the century. Here is an opportunity for spiritual growth through a system of study and practice that is self-propelled, for better or worse, while also being structured and rigorous. Like any other spiritual practice, the effort that one puts into this process is proportional to the benefit it will provide for your life. My advice to you is to savor this material and let it become a part of you while you become a part of it. Allow it to slowly adjust your gaze in this world away from the myopic perspective spoon-fed through tiny electronic screens into the broad and timeless gaze of the ancestors. Here is a modern mysticism, grounded in archaeology and refined by daily practice, that is as timeless as it is renewing; I hope that you find it as compelling and fulfilling as I have.

DR. KENNETH PROEFROCK

KENNETH PROEFROCK, NMD, graduated from Southwest College of Naturopathic Medicine in 1996. He and his wife, Darla, live in the desert of Arizona with numerous snakes, lizards, tortoises, toads, peacocks, dogs, horses, and goats. Prior to naturopathic medical school, he received degrees in chemistry and zoology from Northern Arizona University and worked as a research and development/quality assurance chemist for Procter & Gamble. For the past twenty-seven years, he has conducted a very busy naturopathic medical practice in Surprise, Arizona, where he focuses on pediatric patients with neurological injuries. He is also the president for the North American Board of Naturopathic Examiners (NABNE) and the chairperson for the biochemistry portion of the Naturopathic Physician's Licensing Exam (NPLEX).

Why I Wrote This Book

I have been a Druid since 1984, the year I joined Ár nDraíocht Féin (ADF) after becoming inspired by a summer spent at the Findhorn Community in Scotland and a week on the island of Iona, where I first heard stories about Druids. I appreciated the scholarly focus of ADF but was less interested in the pan-Indo-European approach to Druidism, which claimed Russian Druids, Norse Druids, and Polish Druids as legitimate.

I already had great reverence for the Celts, having been born in Austria and taught by my mother to revere them. Druids were a facet of ancient Celtic culture, especially in Gaul and the insular Celtic areas. The term *Druid* comes down to us from the Gaulish *Druides*, which is from the Celtic compound *dru-wid*, "strong seer," from Old Celtic *derwos*, "true," from the proto-Indo-European (PIE) language root *deru*, "tree," especially Oak, and *wid*, "to know" from the PIE root *weid*, "to see." Thus, a Druid is an Oak knower or Oak seer, meaning a person with solid knowledge, wisdom, and vision as strong and durable as an Oak.

At Pagan Spirit Gathering in 1986, a group of disaffected ADF members including myself, Tony Taylor, his then-wife, Sable, and three others, sat around a campfire and dreamed up a Celtic Druid order (what a concept!). The Henge of Keltria was born. After that I enthusiastically traveled the United States entirely at my own expense, bringing the good news about Keltria to many Pagan venues and festivals. I was eventually elected vice president, a position I held for nine years.

Later, my focus shifted ever deeper into Celtic studies, and I created the White Oak email list on Yahoo in 1996. I pulled together the best Druid minds I was aware of, and we held intense online discussions about what a Druid is and what a Druid isn't for a year. We also crafted a teaching program, basic tools, and book list that would honor the ancient title of Druid by creating knowledgeable and competent clergy who would bring respect to the title.

At the Winter Solstice of 1997, White Oak decided to become a Druid order and twelve of us self-initiated. The entire history of the group's founding and activity is now safely printed out and ensconced in acid-free boxes held at Carleton College in Northfield, Minnesota, exclusively for the benefit of serious scholars. I am deeply indebted to the Druids who participated in the work, both before and after the Order was born. When the Order of the White Oak (Ord na Darach Gile) folded in 2014, I went on to found Tribe of the Oak (Tuatha na Dara) and serve as its Archdruid, just to keep the lessons alive. I recently stepped down as Archdruid, in the summer of 2023, though I am still there to mentor initiates.

As an author I spend a lot of time online, both to teach and to promote my writings. Too often I will see someone asking about Druids—how to become one and where to start on the path—and very often there will be a chorus of "just go sit under a tree," or "spend time in nature and you will be a Druid." While I agree that spending time in nature is at least half of what a genuine Druid does, there is much more to it than that. It seems disrespectful to the ancient Druids, who spent at least twenty years in study to earn the title, to make them out as simple tree huggers.*

In this book I will do my best to share what I have learned about Druids in forty years of study. And I am just a beginner on this path.

---

*See Liam Breatnach's translation of the *Uraicecht na Ríar: The Poetic Grades in Early Irish Law* if you want to appreciate what a Druid Bard was expected to learn, year by year.

Acknowledgments

I wish to thank the White Oak members who had a hand in creating and celebrating our liturgy, rules, rituals and teachings: Dr. Kenneth Proefrock, Donna Lee Urlacher, Brendan Cathbad Myers, Morgan Daimler, Craig Melia, Stacey Weinberger, American poet Merlin Beag (Kevin Moore), Charles Larson, and all the original members of the Order of the White Oak. Alexei Kondratiev was a valued Druid mentor for us as was Searles O'Dubhain in the early days when White Oak was just a Yahoo mailing list.

Thanks are due to Dr. Kenneth Proefrock for the lovely foreword as well as his contribution, "Revelations of Nature." Special appreciation goes to Kate Devlin, Ph.D., for her contributions to the text and art and to Peter J. Quandt for his essay, "Druids and Trees."

PART I

An Introduction to Druidry

Ancient Wisdom and
Modern Knowing

What a Druid Is and Is Not

Gaine daughter of pure Gumor, nurse of mead-loving Mide, surpassed all women though she was silent, she was learned and a seer and a chief Druid.

FROM *THE METRICAL DINDSENCHAS*

How familiar are you with Druidry? You may never even have heard the word *Druid* spoken out loud. Maybe you only read about Druids in a novel or in a comic book. For most people the word *Druid* conjures up a mysterious old man with a beard, working magic in the woods while living as a wise and solitary hermit.

Who Were the Druids?

In reality Druids were both male and female members of the Nemed, or sacred, class. Being part of a caste meant most Druids were likely trained by their parents, although some went to a Druid College if they were not the children of Druids. Despite Victorian fantasies, they would not have led solitary lives as forest hermits because to be a Druid was to provide an essential tribal office. The Druids served the tribe and the ruling class as lawyers, judges, ambassadors, doctors, herbalists, ritualists, historians, genealogists, poets, and a host of other skilled functions.

Druids were the learned class of the ancient Celts, analogous to the Brahmins of India. Druids presided at divinations and sacrifices and praised the Goddesses and Gods. But the primary task of all grades of Druids was to follow an intellectual path. Among Druids there were specialists; it seems unlikely that every Druid presided over every type of function. And Druids did not commit their knowledge to writing; important facts were memorized and passed down orally. (The fact that important things were not written down is a great loss to us moderns. But it did help the Druids to preserve the franchise and prevent others from altering the teachings!)

Both Hindu and Celtic culture are derived from the same proto-Indo-European roots. The caste system of the Hindus (until the Muslim invasions of the ninth century) and the caste system of the ancient Celts were essentially the same—both were fluid; that is, one could move up or down the social ladder depending on skill and learning and depending on one's behavior. Miscreants might find themselves demoted to the pig stye or set out to sea in a coracle without oars, banished from the tribe.

The ancient Celtic societal structure was very similar to what we still see in India today. The Druids were analogous to the Brahmins, the warriors to the Kshatriya. There was the producer class of farmers and craftsmen, and the slaves who were somewhat analogous to the Hindu *Sudra*, the untouchables. Celtic women enjoyed rights that modern women would not see again for almost two thousand years— a woman could inherit land, exercise rights of divorce, and claim the same parental status to a child as its father. If a female slave bore the child of the chieftain, that child had the same status as any other children of the chieftain.

A Druid could be a Sencha, or historian, for the tribe. They could be a Brehon, in which case they would have memorized volumes of law, making them eligible to be a lawyer, a judge, or an ambassador. A Druid could also be a Scelaige, or keeper of sacred myths and epics. These myths were recited at important occasions like weddings and births and at the onset of a major journey or a battle.

The Cainte was a master of magical chants, invocations, and curses.

They could banish or bless with a song. The Cruitire was a harpist who knew the magical uses of music; she was mistress of the three kinds of music: laughing music (the sound of young men at play), crying music (the sound of a woman in the travails of childbirth), and sleeping music (the sound of which would put a person to sleep).

The Druid might be a Liaig, a doctor who used surgery, herbs, and magic to heal, or a Deoghbaire, a cupbearer who knew the properties of intoxicating and hallucinogenic substances. Further specialties included the Faith , or Diviner, the Bard, who was a poet, storyteller, and singer, and the Fili, a sacred poet and diviner whose utterances were prophetic.

As Sorcerers, Druids performed feats of magic in the service of the king or queen and in the service of the tribe. One magical specialty was healing. Another was battle magic, as demonstrated in *Forbhais Droma Damhghaire (The Siege of Knocklong)*. The following is from the Sean O'Duinn translation:

> Then Mogh Roith said to Ceann Mor: "Bring me my poison-stone, my hand-stone, my hundred-fighter, my destruction of my enemies."
>
> This was brought to him, and he began to praise it, and he proceeded to put a venomous spell on it . . .[1]

Druids were the teachers of the sons and daughters of the nobility. It was their task to hand down from generation to generation the knowledge of sacred animals, trees, plants, stones, and all the details of the landscape, its history, and how each feature got its name, as well as the tribal laws and precedents. In contrast to village Cunning Men and Wise Women (Witches), who were counselors, midwives, magicians, herbalists, and veterinarians for the commoners, Druids advised and worked closely with the nobility.

The king or queen was a person from the warrior class who had spent their entire life learning the arts of defense and war and was then elevated to the sacred Nemed class by means of an elaborate ritual.* Druids were hereditary members of the Nemed class who had spent their lives learning the laws and rituals.

A king or queen had to have a Druid advisor by their side at all times so that they could rule according to precedent, and the stories of Arthur and Merlin are a folk memory of this relationship. The fate of the ruler hung on the ability of his or her Druid. There were dire consequences if the ruler failed to judge wisely, and they depended on their Druid advisors to recite the correct laws and precedents. The king's justice was so important that it would determine whether strong and good-looking children would be born to the people, and if the weather, crops, and animals would prosper.

There is evidence that the Druids supervised at human sacrifices or possibly even offered themselves up as a sacrifice for the good of the tribe. However, there is no evidence of the type of wholesale immolation in wicker cages reported by Julius Caesar. It is well to remember that Caesar was attempting to paint the Druids in a lurid light in order to get funding from Rome to continue his military campaigns and to further his personal political ambitions. It seems likely that prisoners of war and criminals were dispatched in much the same way as they are today, after judgment and sentencing. Greek historian Diodorus Siculus, states:

> It's not lawful to offer any sacrifice without a philosopher [Druid] present; for they hold that by these, as men acquainted with the nature of the deity, and familiar with the gods, they ought to present their offerings, and by these ambassadors to desire such things as are good for them. These druids and bards are observed and obeyed, not only in times of peace but war also, both by friends and enemies.[2]

---

*We have at least part of that ritual preserved in the *Audacht Morainn* (Testament of Morann) where a Druid gives advice to a young king. The Fergus Kelly translation is available online in English.

Druids were persecuted by the Romans and killed off in many Celtic areas because the Romans understood that Druids had freedom of movement and would carry intelligence from tribe to tribe. They also saw that Druids performed essential administrative and professional roles within the tribes and if they could eliminate the Druids, the tribes would collapse. However, the Romans never got to the extreme north of Caledonia (Scotland) nor did they invade Ireland. As a result, the Druids and their teachings persisted for many centuries. The Bards were long able to continue to disseminate Druid teachings via story and song.

Who the Druids Were Not

Information found in many New Age and Pagan books, and online, regarding Druids is unreliable. Victorian writers contributed to the confusion with wild opinions about Druidry at a time when archaeology and Celtic studies were still in their infancy. Unfortunately, some of their fantasies persist in the popular mind today.

The Druids were not priests and priestesses of Atlantis, nor were they a lost tribe of Israel. Early English historians could not imagine that groups such as the Irish, whom they considered to be backward and inferior, could possibly have produced a class of noble intellectuals and clergy.

The Druids did not build Stonehenge, nor did they build the magnificent cairns of the Boyne Valley: Knowth, Dowth, and Newgrange. These were built by pre-Indo-European, Late Neolithic, peoples. However, it is quite likely that the Druids used those monuments, just as modern Druids still use them today. In the case of the Irish structures, there is plenty of mythological evidence that the Iron Age Celts and their Druids revered those already venerable sites as sacred.

The ancient Druids were not proto-Christians. They had their own system of ethics and deities that predated Christianity. As the Christian religion gradually took over, Pagan Druids eventually melded with

Christians to form the Culdee—ascetic Christian monastic communities of Ireland, Scotland, Wales, and England. This may have happened because Christian priests and the Druids were both members of a similar class of clergy and intellectuals (the earliest Christian communities held both men and women and were organized very much like a typical Celtic tribe). But there was also a terrible pandemic in 541CE: the Justinianic Plague. Around the same period there were massive climate changes and crop failures. The societal collapse due to those calamities may have pushed the remaining Druids to ally with Christian clergy simply as a means to survival.

It is worth remembering that the Culdee tradition, which is currently making a comeback in Scotland and Ireland, retained a strong element of nature worship in their teachings. All of which brings us to the difficult question of what it means to be a Druid in the modern era.

Who Are Druids Today?

Most modern Druids do attempt to honor Celtic tradition. They also understand that there is no fully intact tradition of Druidism that stretches back to ancient times and that, of necessity, every Druid order must create its own ritual form. Despite claims to the contrary, there are simply no unbroken lineages of Druids still in existence today.

Some Druid orders are happy to include recent speculations, such as the poetry of the English poet Robert Graves (inventor of the Celtic Tree Calendar) and the romantic forgeries of the Welsh *Iolo Morganwg* (Edward Williams, author of *Barddas*). Others stick to more rigorously researched, scholastically verifiable ancient sources such as the *Audacht Morainn*, *Uraicecht Na Riar*, *Bechbretha* (Bee Laws), and *Carmina Gadelica*.

It is more common to find practicing Christians among the English Orders. American Druid orders, such as Tribe of the Oak, the Order of the White Oak, the Henge of Keltria, and ADF, place a larger emphasis on Pagan Celtic scholarship. They see themselves as lore keepers for actual Pagan Celtic cultural, religious, and magical traditions.

Irish Druidism is often concerned with the Forest Druid tradition, seeking to keep alive the ancient woods lore of the forest dwellers of the pre-Elizabethan era. Just about all Druids worldwide care deeply about trees and the fate of the Earth's forests, but because the teachings were an oral tradition and, as a means of protection, not written down. Druids of today are tasked with creating their own unique ritual styles and practices.

As in the past, most modern Druids tend to be intellectually curious, reading voraciously on subjects such as Celtic tribal law, history, philosophy, poetry, magic, religion, mythology, spirituality, traditional healing methods, music, archaeology, and astronomy. They use these studies to create ceremonies that honor the Earth and the Celtic pantheon of Goddesses and Gods.

But when it comes to describing Druids, things quickly become complicated. Druids define themselves in different ways: There are Celtic Reconstructionist Druids who scour the ancient wisdom poetry and texts, archaeology, and Celtic folklore and history to make an attempt at a somewhat historically accurate practice. There are Hedge Druids who believe that each Druid can make it up as they go along, collecting bits of lore and ways of worshipping from disparate sources, Druidic or not, both ancient and recently invented. The old British Romantic Revival Druid groups are heavily influenced by their Masonic founders and history. And Christian Druids retain their reverence for Jesus Christ, even as they adhere to a Polytheist religion. Then there are those who insist that Druidism is not a religion at all, just a philosophy.

Modern Druids are not a male priesthood. There are a few popular authors and at least one old Masonic-style English Order, the Ancient Order of Druids (AOD), that try to perpetuate that idea, but they are in the minority and do not represent the majority of Druids today. That said, it is still relatively rare to find women in positions of leadership among Druids. As detailed in the introduction, I am one of the few women who has co-created, created, and held positions of administrative and spiritual leadership in Druid orders. Emma Restall Orr was once co-chief of the British Druid order, Wren Taylor was Archdruid of the Henge of Keltria, and and Gina McGarry was Archdruid of Tara in Ireland. The British-based Order of Bards, Ovates, and Druids has recently acquired an Irish female Chosen Chief, Eimear Burke. There was also Archdruid Gina McGarry of Tara in Ireland. The Tribe of the Oak now has a new female Archdruid, Melangell Green, and Dana O'Driscoll is the current Grand Archdruid of the Ancient Order of Druids in America. As far as female leadership in Druid orders is concerned, things have recently shown improvement.

That said, most Druid groups have roughly the same number of female and male members, in contrast to other Pagan paths such as Witchcraft and Wicca, which seem to be more heavily populated by and led by women.

What Do Druids Do?

Druids recognize that nature hangs in a delicate balance and that all life must be tended with care. They engage in Earth-friendly activities such as recycling, eating organic produce, planting trees, and tending their own organic gardens.

Druids do not ignore the needs of the people. As in ancient times they care for the welfare of their community, giving comfort in times of sickness and death, rejoicing in each other's life passages and achievements, and seeking to advise, as best they can, the secular leaders of their towns, states, and nations. They donate time and money to religious, cultural, environmental, and humanitarian projects that capture their imaginations.

In short, Druidism is not a solitary path. Even if practicing alone (because there are so few of us it is often not possible to circle with other Druids without traveling a great distance), the Druid is not isolated from nature, her spiritual community, her town, her city, her nation, or the world.

So How Do Druids Worship?

Druids love nature and seek to know the land they live on intimately, observing seasonal and astronomical changes and animal behaviors as timing for festivals and as portents for the future. The most important holy days for Druids are the four fire festivals: Samhain, Imbolc, Beltaine, and Lughnasad (there is more about these important Celtic holidays later in the book). Each fire festival begins in the evening because the ancient Celts reckoned that the day starts at dusk. Many Druids also celebrate the sky festivals or astronomical observances such as equinoxes and solstices, and some meet at the full or new Moon.

The Earth-aligned high holy days for Druids are: Samhain (October 31–November 1), the official end of the harvest, the start of the new year, and a time to honor the beloved dead; Imbolc (February 1–2), the advent of spring and essentially a milk festival—the celebration of the lactation of the ewes who give milk again at this time; Beltaine (April 30–May 1), marked by the blooming of the Hawthorn tree, which tells us it is warm enough to send cows up to their hillside pastures; and Lughnasad (July 31–August 1), the beginning of the harvest when the first fruits are taken and thanks are given.

Druids honor rivers, trees, mountains, herbs, rocks, animals, and every living thing. Druids recognize an inward Spirit within all creation, an intelligence that can be accessed and consulted whenever wisdom is needed. Old trees and large stones are perceived as having a depth of spiritual knowledge, as are bodies of water such as lakes, ponds, streams, and the ocean. Animals including deer, bears, wolves, salmon, eagles, boar, horses, owls, whales, cats and dogs, butterflies, bees, and dragonflies are seen to carry messages from Spirit. White Oak Druids and Tribe of the Oak Druids take an oath to protect the Earth and

Her creatures and make offerings of thanks to fire, water, trees, stones, and the local River Goddess of the Druid's bioregion, in keeping with ancient Indo-European tradition.

Druids place a greater emphasis on praising the Goddesses and Gods and less of a focus on magic; they use song, poetry, and crafts to express their love and kinship with their chosen deities and Spirit Animals.

Celtic Reconstructionist Druids work with the Three Worlds (Land, Sea, and Sky) more than the Four Directions. If we do call in directions it will be at least five, including the Sacred Center, or as many as twelve, based on the ancient Airts, or winds.

Druids invoke and thank the ancestors, the Nature Spirits, and the Goddesses and Gods in their rites. The Realm of Sea is understood to be under the Earth. This is where the ancestors and Fairies dwell; offerings to them are given to water or poured onto the soil because the liquid carries the offerings down to their realm. Gifts to the Nature Spirits are spread upon the land, given to a tree, or placed on a stone or outdoor altar. Offerings to Goddesses and Gods are placed into a fire because the flames carry the offerings upward to the Sky Realm where the deities reside.

Druids are true polytheists, understanding each deity as a distinct individual with His or Her unique likes, dislikes, and spheres of influence. Among Druids it is considered somewhat rude to bring deities from different religions and cultures together into the same circle, and every effort is made to work within genuine Celtic pantheons. Many of us also recognize Sacred Source, the ineffable place from which all creation, including deities, emanates. Thus, we can be monotheist, polytheist, and animist—all at the same time!

A Witch's circle is a closed space, designed to hold and contain energy to build it into a cone of power. A Druid circle is a permeable affair; persons and pets may walk in and out at will. Since part of the energy raising involves inviting the Nature Spirits to participate, Druids feel that there is no point in walling off the circle.

Druid ceremonies are most often performed out of doors, ideally in the presence of living water, a fire, and a tree (or a large standing stone, pole, or staff substitute). Modern Druids do not practice animal or human sacrifice and instead regard hard work, charity, and artistic achievement as adequate offerings. That said, there are many different Druid orders, and as is the case with most Pagan groupings, no two Druids will see things in exactly the same light. As someone once put it to me, Paganism is a "conversational religion," and our discussions about what to do and how to do it are endless, especially considering the different focus and feel to American Druid orders and to Irish or English ones. I can only speak for myself, as an American Druid of the Order of the White Oak (Ord Na Darach Gile) and of the Tribe of the Oak (Tuatha na Dara).

Historical Knowledge
about the Druids

Julius Caesar is probably the source most people are familiar with when it comes to describing Druids. He wrote in *The Conquest of Gaul*:

> The Druids officiate at the worship of the gods, regulate public and private sacrifices, and give rulings on all religious questions. Large numbers of young men flock to them for instruction, and they are held in great honour by the people. They act as judges in practically all disputes, whether between tribes or between individuals; when any crime is committed, or a murder takes place, or a dispute arises about an inheritance or a boundary, it is they who adjudicate the matter and appoint the compensation to be paid and received by the parties concerned. Any individual or tribe failing to accept their award is banned from taking part in sacrifice—the heaviest punishment that can be inflicted upon a Gaul. Those who are laid under such a ban are regarded as impious criminals. Everyone shuns them and avoids going near or speaking to them, for fear of taking some harm by contact with what is unclean; if they appear as plaintiffs, justice is denied them, and they are excluded from a share in any honour. All the Druids are under one head, whom they hold in the highest respect. On his death, if any one of the rest is of outstanding merit,

14

he succeeds the vacant place; if several have equal claims, the Druids
usually decide the election by voting, though sometimes they actually
fight it out. On a fixed date each year they hold a session in a consecrated spot in the country of the Carnutes, which is supposed to be
the centre of Gaul. Those who are involved in disputes assemble here
from all parts, and accept the Druids' judgements and awards. The
Druidic doctrine is believed to have been found existing in Britain
and thence imported into Gaul; even today those who want to make a
profound study of it generally go to Britain for the purpose.[1]

From this account we can see that there must have been at least
some uniformity of practice and belief among the Druids of Gaul,
Britain, and Ireland since Druids made an effort to go to Britain (most
likely Wales) for their training. Caesar further states:

The Druids are exempt from military service and do not pay taxes
like other citizens. These important privileges are naturally attractive: many present themselves of their own accord to become
students of Druidism, and others are sent by their parents or
relatives. It is said that these pupils have to memorize a great number of verses—so many, that some of them spend twenty years at
their studies. The Druids believe that their religion forbids them
to commit their teachings to writing, although for most other purposes, such as public and private accounts, the Gauls use the Greek
alphabet. But I imagine that this rule was originally established for
other reasons—because they did not want their doctrine to become
public property, and in order to prevent their pupils from relying on
the written word and neglecting to train their memories; for it is
usually found that when people have the help of texts, they are less
diligent in learning by heart, and let their memories rust. A lesson
which they take particular pains to inculcate is that the soul does
not perish, but after death passes from one body to another; they
think that this is the best incentive to bravery, because it teaches

men to disregard the terrors of death. They also hold long discussions about the heavenly bodies and their movements, the size of the universe and of the earth, the physical constitution of the world, and the power and properties of the gods; and they instruct the young men in all these subjects.[2]

In this description we read that the Druids knew Greek letters but passed down their own teachings orally. They taught the doctrine of reincarnation and were astronomers, naturalists, and religious specialists. We can also deduce the high status that Irish Druids once held from other accounts:

> The druid (Old Irish druí) was priest, prophet, astrologer, and teacher of the sons of nobles. According to the sixth century *First Synod of Saint Patrick* oaths were sworn in his presence . . . . Their magic spells were certainly feared: an eighth century hymn asks God for protection from the spells of women, blacksmiths and druids. They may also have concocted the love-potions which are mentioned in law-texts and other sources. Some of their sorcery was effected through *corrguinecht*, a term which seems to mean "heron (or crane) killing," and apparently involved the recitation of a satire standing on one leg with one arm raised and one eye shut (in imitation of a heron's stance?). The druids' power could be useful in war. The *Annals of Ulster* s.a. 560 = 561 (marginal addition of later date) record the use of a druid fence (*erbe ndruad*) in the battle of Cúil Dremne. Any warrior who leaped over it was killed. According to the *Bretha Nemed toísech*, a druid can ensure victory for the weaker side in battle.[3]

By the time the Brehon Laws, early Irish legislation, which are discussed in detail later, were written down by monks in the seventh to eighth centuries (they were oral before that), Druids had been demoted to the status of magician or sorcerer, due to the Christian conversions.

What Did Druids Wear?

This question is important for those of us who design and perform Druidic rituals. Druid clergy, especially, usually make an effort to look somewhat "Iron Age" as they enact their religious role.

The ancient Druids probably had a distinguishing costume like most priestly castes, but the ancient sources we have are slender. We're told by the Roman writer and philosopher Pliny the Elder that they wore white during the New Moon Mistletoe-cutting ceremony, and medieval Irish sources speak of the *tuigen*—a "covering" that at least some Druids wore, which seems to refer to a robe with feathers, a typical shamanic costume.

We do know that they had a specific transverse tonsure—shaving the hair in front of a line drawn over the top of the head from ear to ear. A term of respect for a Druid or poet was *shining brow*, possibly in reference to this tonsure. For example, Taliesin of the Shining Brow is a mytho-historical character associated with early Wales and Britain in the sixth century CE.

The following entry from *The Annals of the Four Masters* tells us something about the colors that were worn:

> This was the first year of Eochaidh Eadghadhach, as king over Ireland. He was called Eochaidh Eadghadhach because it was by him the variety of colour was first put on clothes in Ireland, to distinguish the honour of each by his raiment, from the lowest to the highest. Thus was the distinction made between them: one colour in the clothes of slaves; two in the clothes of soldiers; three in the clothes of goodly heroes, or young lords of territories; six in the clothes of ollavs; seven in the clothes of kings and queens.[4]

The Ollav was a high grade of Druid, one who had fully mastered a specialty and was teaching it to others. In modern parlance they would be called a Doctor of Philosophy (Ph.D.). Here we see that the Ollav was entitled to wear six colors. The number of colors that you wore was your calling card, everyone knew your status the moment they saw you, based on the colors of your clothing.

According to Geoffrey Keating's (also known as Seathrún Céitinn) *The History of Ireland*, written around 1632, Tighernmas (Milesian King of Ireland, circa 900 BCE) is said to have introduced the colors purple, blue, and green to Ireland from his trading with the Phoenicians.[5] This king was also said to have established the numbers and types of colors that could be worn by the different classes of Irish society. Keating lists the acceptable colors as one color in the dress of a slave, two in the dress of a peasant, three in the dress of a soldier or young lord, four in the dress of a *brughaidh* (landholder), five in the dress of a district chief, six in the dress of an Ollav, and seven in that of a king and queen.

Entries under *breacan* (a highland plaid or tartan plaid) in both Edward Dwelly's *Illustrated Gaelic-English Dictionary*, published in early 1900s, and Norman MacLeod and Daniel Dewar's 1866 *A Dictionary of the Gaelic Language in Two Parts* note that these were worn from the earliest Celtic days and that the variety of colors represented the rank of

Figure 1. The author in Celtic garb.
Photo by Justin Fisher.

the wearer. The ancient kings wore seven colors, Druids wore six, and nobles were restricted to four colors.

So, there does seem to be agreement that Druids did not wear the Egyptian-style hooded white robes that we moderns often imagine (except maybe for the Mistletoe-rite, possibly in honor of the white berries born by that plant) and that they probably wore colorful plaids and shamanic-style feathered cloaks.

What Other Accessories Could a Druid Be Expected to Carry?

At least one burial thought to have been of a Druid contained perforated "spoons" similar to implements used for libations in Vedic rituals. These may have been normal accessories for a Druid.

A Druid would probably have carried some form of knife or sickle for the harvesting of sacred plants, especially if they were a healer.

Archaeologists have also uncovered a burial with surgical instruments as well as what might have been divination rods. The herb Artemisia (most likely mugwort but possibly wormwood or a mixture of both) was discovered in a bowl found in the same burial, which points to a familiarity with herbal remedies and healing and suggests the roles of both magic and medicine.[6]

Were Druids Warriors?

While we do have some stories of warrior-Druids, such as Fionn mac Cumhaill (Finn MacCool) of the Fianna, who was raised by both a female Druid and a female warrior, it would have been exceedingly rare for a Druid to act as a warrior in battles. Druids were ambassadors, arbiters of treaties, and peace brokers, meaning they had to be beyond the fray to be able to negotiate with both sides.

Also, a Druid spent twenty or more years in study memorizing laws, stories, poems, and genealogies, meaning there wasn't much time to perfect the arts of killing and battle. That was the specialty of the warrior class and of the king who had to be ritually elevated to Nemed status after an education in the arts of war.

All hostilities ceased the moment a Druid stepped onto a battlefield because each Druid was a walking library of knowledge, laws, and precedents. To harm or kill a Druid would have been like burning down a library! However, we do know that some Druids practiced battle magic on behalf of their warrior kings. The Greek historian Diodorus Siculus, born in the first century BCE, remarked:

> Many times these philosophers and poets, stepping in between two near at hand, when they are just ready to engage, with their swords drawn, and spears presented one against another, have pacified them, as if some wild beasts had been tamed by enchantments. Thus rage is mastered by wisdom, even amongst the most savage barbarians, and Mars himself reverences the Muses.[7]

Did Druids Get Married?

As part of the Nemed class, like the Brahmins of India, they most probably married, but some may have remained celibate for ritual reasons.

Did the Druids Practice Magic?

I think we can be pretty sure that the Druids practiced magic, bearing in mind that certain arts such as herbal healing and smithcraft were considered to be magic in those days. Here are some of the magical arts of the Tuatha Dé Danann—a highly skilled supernatural race known as the people or tribe of the Goddess Danu who ruled Ireland before the arrival of the Celtic Milesians—and their Druids, as set forth in the *Cath Maige Tuired* (The Second Battle of Moytura):

> Foglaim feasa (occult lore)
> Fithasachta (sorcery)

Druidechtai (Druidic arts)
Amaidechtai (Witchcraft)
Amainsechtai (magical skill)
Cerd ngenntlichtae (Pagan arts)

These are the Druidic arts of the Tuatha Dé Danann from *Lebor Gabála Érenn* (The Book of Invasions), Section VII:

Druidechta (Druidry)
Fessa (Knowledge)
Fástini (Prophecy)
Amainsechtai (Magic)
Cerdaib Suithe Gentliuchta (Arts of Pagan Cunning)

Were All Druids Old Men with Beards?

Despite what Julius Caesar wrote, there is evidence of female Druids, or *bandruid*, in Irish mythology. Three Druidesses are named in the Táin (The Cattle Raid of Cooley) and in *The Siege of Knocklong* and two in the *Dinsenchas*. Mythological accounts also refer to an Alba (Britain)-trained female poet, or *banfili*, in Queen Mebd of Connacht's court. *The Annals of Innisfallen* for the year 934 discuss the death of the "woman poet of Ireland." The Brehon Laws, however, detail harsh penalties for illegally practicing female satirists, comparing them to werewolves. So although the trope of the old man with a white beard is pervasive, the role of Druid and poet was not entirely patriarchal.

This is just some of the evidence we have that there were indeed female Druids. In modern times, Druids are about half males and half females.

Who Were the Bards?

From the account of James Bonwick in *Old Irish Religions*, we can deduce the depth of learning involved in becoming a Bard. It wasn't just a matter of entertaining people with songs and stories in an ale house. He writes:

> The Irish Bards proper occupied a high position in Ireland. The Ollamhs had colleges at Clogher, Armagh, Lismore, and Tamar. On this, *Walker's Historical Memoirs*, 1786, observes that "all the eminent schools, delectably situated, which were established by the Christian clergy in the fifth century, were erected on the ruins of those colleges."
>
> They studied for twelve years to gain the barred cap and title of Ollamh, or teacher. They were Ollamhain Redan, or Filidhe, poets. They acted as heralds, knowing the genealogy of their chiefs. With white robe, harp in hand, they encouraged warriors in battle. Their power of satire was dreaded; and their praise, desired.
>
> Brehons—Breitheamhain—were legislative Bards; and, said Walker, in 1786, they "promulgated the laws in a kind of recitative, or monotonous chant, seated on an eminence in the open air." According to McCurtin, the Irish Bards of the sixth century wore long, flowing garments, fringed and ornamented with needlework. In *Life of Columba*, 1827, it is written, "The Bards and Sennachees retained their office, and some degree of their former estimation among the nobility of Caledonia and Ireland, till the accession of the House of Hanover."[8]

Exploring Some Celtic and Hindu Parallels

Another way to understand who the Druids might have been is to read Vedic and Hindu scriptures and to explore what parallels we can find from archaeology.

In modern times the holiest river of Hinduism is the Ganges. But before the Ganges became the focus of religious belief and ritual there was another river that was likely equally sacred. That river was the Sarasvati, around which an entire civilization known as the Harappan culture flourished from 2500 BCE to 1500 BCE in the Indus River Valley of present-day northwest India and Kashmir. Its major cities were Harappa and Mohenjo-Daro.

The Harappan culture was highly advanced with writing, mathematics, metallurgy, dentistry, stringed instruments, three-dimensional sculptures, urban planning, irrigation and drainage, public baths, and boats and canals. It had a population that was larger than the two kingdoms of northern and southern Egypt combined. It was a culture that traded widely and lived in peace. Their language was most likely a type of Dravidian.[9]

This culture faced an environmental catastrophe when the climate changed. The rains failed, and their sacred Mother River, the Sarasvati, dried up. By approximately 2000 BCE the holy river that had run through the heart of this civilization was gone and the Harappan culture began to disperse. What remained of the Harrapan culture was absorbed or conquered by proto-Indo-European or Sanskrit speakers.

Evidence suggests that some of these Harappan peoples moved south, into the subcontinent, from Northwest India, while other Harappans moved northeast into China and Tibet. There is also mounting evidence that yet others of them may have moved west—all the way into Western Europe.

What evidence do we have to support this theory? As physical evidence we have the famous Gundestrup Cauldron that was found in a Danish bog in 1891. The provenance for the cauldron is still debated but it was constructed in the first or second century BCE. Despite coming from a Danish bog, the cauldron depicts a horned deity seated in a yogic pose, surrounded by exotic creatures (see figure 2 on page 24).

The horned deity is clearly Celtic; we know this because he is

Figure 2. Detail from the Gundestrup Cauldron.

The Gundestrup Cauldron is housed in the National Museum of Denmark (Nationalmuseet). This image was provided to Wikimedia Commons by Nationalmuseet as part of an ongoing cooperative project under CC BY-SA 3.0.

Figure 3. The Pashupati seal, showing a seated and possibly tricephalic figure, surrounded by animals.
Circa 2350–2000 BCE. Public domain.

wearing a torc (neck ring), which is a Celtic symbol of noble status, and he holds another torc in his hand. Yet the horned figure closely resembles the Harrapan Mohenjo-Daro depictions of Shiva Pasupathi, the Lord of the Animals (see figure 3).

In Hindu depictions of Shiva he is often shown meditating with a serpent around his neck to illustrate his absolute fearlessness. Similarly, the Gundestrup horned deity is shown clutching a serpent.

Other parallels can be found between European, Vedic, and Indus Valley cultures. The sacred mother river called the Danube, along which European Celtic culture possibly developed, is named for the Celtic Goddess Danu. The same Goddess gave her name to other rivers including the Don River and the Dnieper. Danu is also an early Hindu Goddess of the primeval waters. In the *Rig Veda* she is called the Mother of the Danavas or the Children of Danu.

As previously mentioned, Celtic peoples developed a caste system with the Nemed, who were the equivalent of Brahmins, warriors equivalent to the Kshatriyas, farmers and producers, and slaves who did the same menial tasks as the untouchable castes of India. In common with Hindu and Vedic cultures where, until the ninth century, one could move up or down the social ladder, advancing in status as one gained education or skills, the ancient Celtic caste system was fluid, providing opportunities for advancement but also loss of status depending upon education and other circumstances.

The Celts and Hindu-Vedic peoples shared other similarities, such as the primacy of triple deities. In Celtic religious thought the most powerful deities were always personified in threes, for example the triple Brighid, who was the most popular pan-Celtic Goddess and who was personified as three Brighids: Brighid the patroness of smiths and the forge, Brighid the patroness of healing, and Brighid the patroness of poets. Similarly, there was Lugh Samildanach, the God who was master of every art, born as one of triplets. The Triple War Goddess known as the Morrígan was often personified as three ravens, three crows, or three great queens named Macha, Badb, and Nemain. The Land Goddess of ancient Ireland was a triple deity: Banba, Fodla and Ériu. In Celtic Gaul the Matronae were the Triple Mothers who brought the blessings of plants, food, and healthy children to the tribes. Thus, the number three implied High Goddesses and Gods, divinity, and completion. These triple deities can be compared to the Hindu Trimurti—Brahma, Shiva, and Vishnu—and to the Tridevi—Saraswati, Lakshmi, and Parvati.

Druidic religious and philosophical teachings were similar to Vedic and Hindu beliefs as well. The Druids taught the doctrine of rebirth according to contemporary witnesses and historians. Pomponius Mela, a Roman geographer who wrote in about 43 CE, reported that the Druids taught reincarnation to strengthen the courage of the warriors. He states:

> One of their dogmas has become widely known so they may the more readily go to wars: namely that souls are everlasting, and that among the shades is another life.

Ammianus Marcellinus, a Roman soldier and historian (330–400 CE), wrote:

> The Druids . . . declared souls to be immortal.

And Diodorus Siculus, an ancient Greek historian born in 90 BCE, declared that:

> The Pythagorean doctrine prevails among them, teaching that the souls of men are immortal and live again for a fixed number of years inhabited in another body.

And in the first century, Marcus Annaeus Lucanus (39–65 CE), better known in English as Lucan, was a Roman poet who addressed the Druids rhetorically with these words:

> You tell us that the same spirit has a body again elsewhere, and that death, if what you sing is true, is but the midpoint of long life.

We can find yet more parallels between the sacred scriptures of the Celtic and Hindu religions. In R. A. Stewart Macalister's translation of *Lebor Gabála Érenn* (The Book of the Taking of Ireland or The Book of Invasions), a book composed of a mixture of pseudohistory and oral lore passed down through the generations, in The Verse Texts section, the poet declares:

> *I am Wind on Sea,*
> *I am the Ocean-wave,*
> *I am the Roar of Sea,*
> *I am Bull of Seven Fights,*
> *I am Vulture on Cliff,*
> *I am Dewdrop,*
> *I am Fairist of Flowers,*
> *I am Boar for Boldness,*
> *I am Salmon in Pool,*
> *I am Lake on Plaain,*
> *I am Mountain in a Man,*
> *I am a Word of Skill,*
> *I am the Point of a Weapon (that*
> *   poureth forth combat),*
> *I am God who fashioneth Fire for a*
> *   Head [i.e. a giver of inspiration] . . .*[10]

This can be compared to the *Bhagavad-Gita* where Sri Krishna says:

> *I am the Self established in the heart of all*
> *   contingent beings:*
> *I am the beginning, the middle, and the end*
> *   of all contingent beings too . . .*[11]

And in the same vein Sri Krishna says:

> *. . . Among luminous bodies I am the sun . . .*
> *among heavenly mansions I am the moon . . .*
> *and Meru among the high-aspiring mountains . . .*
> *of floods I am the ocean . . .*
> *of immovable things I am the Himalaya . . .*
> *I am the lion among beasts . . .*
> *the Ganges among rivers . . .*
> *I am endless time itself, and the Preserver whose face*
>   *is turned on all sides . . .*
> *I am, O Arjuna, the seed of all existing things,*
>   *and there is not anything, whether animate or*
>   *inanimate which is without me . . .*[12]

Added to all this is the fact that Celtic religion featured offerings to sacred fire, sacred water, and sacred trees, while Vedic ritual involved making offerings to sacred fire (Agni), and sacred water (Soma) and the use of a pole in their rites. The sickle was a ritual implement used by both Druids and Brahaminic priests. The evidence is mounting that there is likely a common Vedic or proto-Vedic thread that runs through Indo-European religious belief.

Goddesses and Gods
of the Druids

To worship the Gods, to do no evil
And to exercise fortitude.
TRIAD OF THE DRUIDS, DIOGENES LAERTIUS

I have been a devotee of the Goddess Brighid for over thirty years. A hand-carved wooden statue of her stands on my altar, surrounded by candles, acorns, and other sacred objects. She is the one who has inspired my writings and pushed me to teach and to speak about Druidism.

Figure 4. Hand-carved wooden statue of the Goddess Brighid on my home altar.
Author's personal photo.

I also have a Brighid Well behind the house, deep in the Oak forest. To get there I walk a narrow woodland trail, then come to a little stream that has a number of pools and small waterfalls built into it with rocks. My Druid Grove has made offerings of coins, flowers, and fruits, and sung to the Well, for over thirty years. There is a small rag tree overhanging the Well where we tie our *clooties* (small strips of cloth) after dipping them into the water and pressing them to any part of our body that is ailing. As the rags decompose, so do our troubles.

This type of holy well is known as a "rag tree" in Ireland or a "clootie well" in Scotland (*clootie* means "little cloth" in Scots). These types of wells have been in use in Celtic areas and in England for millennia. Originally the wells were sacred to Celtic deities but after the Christian conversions became reconsecrated to Christian saints. The classic configuration for such a well is water, an associated stone or stones, and an overhanging tree, typically a Hawthorn or an Ash.

Crossing the stream, I climb a small hill in the forest that came

Figure 5. The well where we place our offerings on the holy days.
Photo by Justin Fisher.

Figure 6. Clooties hanging from a tree over a stream behind the house.
Photo by Justin Fisher.

complete with a natural circle of stones. There is now a fire pit in the center. Looking up at the Oak leaves and the sky beyond feels like gazing at an elaborate, green, stained-glass window that is set in a vast open-air cathedral. This is the place where we make our offerings to the Celtic deities by placing gifts to them into the fire. The fire carries the offerings upward, to the Sky Realm, the abode of the High Goddesses and Gods.

Bonding with Celtic Deities

As a Druid you will naturally want to forge your own connection with one or more Celtic deities. For Druids our relationship with the Goddesses and Gods is a reciprocal affair. We make offerings to them on the high holy days and on other important occasions, and they reciprocate by inspiring and guiding us through dreams, divinations, and signs.

If you are just starting out on this path, you may not yet have a divine patron or patroness to collaborate with. Be patient, because over time a deity will *choose you*. There is no need to worry about this. A deity will come to you eventually, and when they do, you will *know*. Once that happens you can make gifts to them of music, poetry, and song and place artworks or gifts of food into the fire for them (because the flames carry the offerings to the Sky Realm). Or, put offerings of flowers, fruits, crafts, or silver into water, or on the earth, in their honor. You can light a candle for them, offer incense, or even set a place at the table for them on the high holy days and at feasts.

We know the names of over four hundred Goddesses and Gods of the Celts. Most of the names are from inscriptions, and a few come down to us from traditional stories. For others we have statues and carved altars as evidence.

We Druids do not grovel or debase ourselves before our Goddesses and Gods. We do not apologize for "sins" nor do we kneel in submission. We see our Goddesses and Gods as shining examples of what we ourselves may become, if we apply ourselves with courage and passion. The goal of the Druid worshipper is to be *just like them*.

For example, someone studying to become a jeweler and goldsmith might maintain an altar in honor of Lugh and seek to master her craft as skillfully as he mastered it. A blacksmith might dedicate his forge to the Fire Goddess Brighid, so that her inspiration will guide his imagination and hands. A farmer might petition a Land Goddess such as Anu, in hope that her energy and guidance will help him to coax life from the soil.

Groups of skilled craftspeople and artisans worshipped the same deities, making them members of a type of guild. Druids would have worshipped Goddesses and Gods such as An Daghda, the Good God and learned leader, to guide and inspire them. Healers would have honored Dian Cecht or Brighid. And so on.

Gender Balance among the Goddesses and Gods

The Celtic Goddesses and Gods have relatively gender-balanced functions. This does not mean the Goddesses and Gods are gender-fluid, rather it implies that the Celts had respect for both sexes. For example, while the Sun, Greine (Sun-Gold-Grain), is regarded as female in Irish lore, we also have Belenos, later known as Beli Mawr (the Great), who is a Celtic God of the Sun. The Dagda with his inexhaustible Cauldron of Plenty is an Earth and Nature God who feeds the people, while the great Mother Earth and River Goddesses Anu/Ana and Danu/Dana lend their fertility to the flocks and the land.

Lugh and Brighid were the most popular pan-Celtic deities and were worshipped by tribes across many regions. Both of these deities are fiery and bright, Master and Mistress of Arts. As a culture the ancient Celts obviously valued sound craftsmanship, intelligence, and poetic inspiration. Brighid's sphere includes poetry, music, smithcraft, healing, and motherhood (to be a mother is to be of necessity a mistress of every art!), while Lugh's domain includes goldsmithing, storytelling, magic, warriorship, and many other arts.

In the healing realm we have Brighid and also the herbalist Airmid, daughter of Dian Cécht. Among male healers we have Dian Cécht and his son Miach.

There are both male and female divinities who guide, empower, and inspire the warriors. The Morrígan is a prominent triple Goddess of Battle associated with ravens and crows. She is a mistress of battle magic and of shape-shifting who lends her energy to combatants. Heroic Gods such as Bran and Lugh are also associated with crows and ravens and help warriors to find strength and success in battle.

The Dagda is the great Father God and patron of the Druids. Brighid is the great Fire Goddess who is patroness of the poets and Bards.

For magicians we have Cerridwen, a Mistress of Magic and shape changing with her great Cauldron of Transformation. Manannán

MacLir is a shapeshifter and Master Magician who opens and closes the veils between the Worlds.

Triple deities are a characteristic of the Indo-European High Goddesses and Gods. But it should be noted that there was no "Maiden-Mother-Crone" anywhere in Celtic thinking (or in any other ancient Pagan religion for that matter). That triplicity is a very modern idea invented by the English poet Robert Graves that seems to categorize Goddesses (and women) by their biological breeding state as virgin, mother, or post-menopausal crone. Celtic Goddesses were far more accomplished than that. In ancient times a Goddess such as Brighid or the Morrígan was triple, meaning three Goddesses in one who are sisters of the same age, because she was understood to be so powerful that she was the equivalent of three "average" Goddesses. Coventina was a triple Maiden Goddess who was worshipped at a holy well near Hadrian's Wall in Scotland. The Matronae were the powerful Triple Mothers who bestowed food and babies, and so on.

Below are just a few of the better-known deities of Celtic tradition, inscriptions, and historical accounts.

The Goddesses

The following descriptions of some of the Goddesses that Druids work with are by no means exhaustive, and if one of these deities calls to you, you should explore her nature and attributes in depth. Reading the traditional stories and meditating on their meaning will make her presence more fully known to you.

The Celts had no "Love Goddesses" per se because every Goddess was assumed to be fertile and sexual, although some Goddesses were described as more amorous or affectionate than others. When a Goddess was triple, she was described as three sisters or three powerful aspects of the same Goddess. Celtic Goddesses usually appeared on their own, without a male consort. You will read about divine pairs, but they were few.

Many Celtic Goddesses had animal attributes. War Goddesses were associated with carrion birds and Goddesses of fertility, maternity, and sovereignty with mares. River Goddesses were associated with cows and spring Goddesses often appeared holding serpents (a symbol of healing). There were horned Goddesses as well as horned Gods.

The Celtic Goddess could be a mother, warrior, crone, or a bestower of fertility. She had a powerful sexual appetite and could be the giver of bounty to the land and the waters, protectress of the flocks and herds, Mistress of Healing, or patroness of the Bards and poets. From her active, powerful, and passionate figure, we gain a sense of what the Celts most admired as feminine attributes.

The Great Triple Goddesses

In Indo-European traditions the High Goddesses and Gods are triple. When we see an image of a Triple Goddess—three aspects of a single Goddess who combine to make a deity with three times the power of a typical Goddess—or a poetic description of one, we know we are dealing with the highest aspects of divinity. Offerings to these High Goddesses and Gods are given to fire because fire carries the offerings up to the Sky Realm where they dwell.

Brighid or Brigid

Known as Brigantia in Britain, as Brigindo in Gaul, and worshipped in all Celtic areas, she was the most popular pan-Celtic Goddess. Some scholars believe she was originally an Indo-European Dawn Goddess or a Sun Goddess. Her name means "exalted one," and she was a Goddess of Fire, associated with the Imbolc festival and the return of the fires of life and light in the spring. As patroness of the Druids and Bards she inspired the fires of creativity in musicians, healers, and poets. As patroness of smiths she inspired the magic of the forge-fire. She was also associated with motherhood and cows (her mother was Boann, the great Cow Goddess of the Boyne River and of the Milky Way) and with the Sun, as she was the Goddess who ushered in the warmth of summer. As a patroness of healers, healing wells were often dedicated to her. Her priestesses once kept a perpetual fire into which they scryed as a means of divining answers for the people. Christian nuns later adopted the practice at Saint Brigid's Fire Temple in Kildare, Ireland, where nuns took turns tending the fire for nineteen days. On the twentieth day Brighid herself tended the flames. The Fire Temple survived up to the suppression of the monasteries in the sixteenth century. Recently nuns have relit the flame and, happily, the tradition continues.

From an old Scottish verse,

> *The serpent will come from the hole*
> *On the brown Day of Bride,*
> *Though there should be three feet of snow*
> *On the flat surface of the ground.* ·

Coventina

Coventina was a Romano-British Goddess of wells and springs. She was known from multiple inscriptions at one site in Northumberland

Figure 7. Coventina as a Triple Nymph on a leaf.

Woodcut published in The Legendary Lore of the Holy Wells of England Including Rivers, Lakes, Fountains and Springs *by Robert Charles Hope, 1893. Public domain.*

County, England, an area surrounding a wellspring near Carrawburgh on Hadrian's Wall where she appears as a Triple Nymph or as a Water Nymph reclining on a leaf, pouring water from a vessel (see figure 7). Votive offerings to Coventina once included coins, brooches, rings, pins, glassware, and pottery.

Ériu

The land of Éire (Ireland) was Herself a Triple Goddess. Ériu, Banba, and Fodla together were the great triple Land Goddess whom the Celt-Iberian Sons of Mil had to overcome to settle in Ireland. In exchange for their colonization, Ériu asked that her name be given to the island, which it carries to this day. Ériu sometimes appears as a gray-white crow.

The Matronae or Matres (Triple Divine Mothers)

When Julius Caesar wrote his famous description of Gaul, he seems to have deliberately left out the most all-pervasive deities of the land,

Figure 8. A Roman sculpture of the Matres (the Triple Divine Mothers).
Housed in Corinium Museum, Cirencester. Photo by Tony Grist. Public domain.

the Triple Mothers, perhaps to make the Celts less sympathetic to his Roman audience. As stated previously, Caesar was seeking funding for his military and political ambitions, and he wasn't interested in portraying the Celts as magnanimous. The Matronae governed fertility and childbirth and were especially pervasive throughout Germania and Gaul. The Matres (Mothers) were also worshipped in Celt-Iberia.

The Morrígan

A triple Goddess whose three sister aspects were Nemain (terror), Macha (plain), and Badb Catha (Battle Raven), she influenced the outcome of battles by her magic and, if inspired, would strike terror into warriors' hearts, depriving them of the will to win. At times she appeared as three hags or as three beautiful young women. She might also appear as three crows or ravens. She would shape-shift into an eel, a wolf, or a heifer to attack any man who refused her sexual advances and at times appeared as a woman by a stream, washing the blood off the weapons and armor of warriors who were about to die.

Great Goddesses of the Land

The land is considered sacred by all Indigenous peoples. Without the dependable bounty of the land, we would not be able to survive. The Land Goddesses were often viewed as fertile beings of great power who fed the people every day.

Áine

An Irish Earth Goddess associated with love, fertility, crops, animals, and summer Sun. She was the daughter of Éogabul, a foster son of Manannán MacLir. Áine was especially venerated as a Fairy Queen in County Limerick while Áine Clí (Bright Áine) was a Sovereignty Goddess in Munster. The Feast of Midsummer Night was held in Áine's honor. She was said to live in the hill now called Cnoc Áine in County Limerick. At Summer Solstice farmers would light *cliars*—

bunches of straw and hay tied on poles—that they carried in procession to the top of the hill. Later, the men ran the clíars through their fields and between the cattle to bring good luck for the rest of the year. Aine would appear as a red mare running through the fields to bless them (mares and horses are associated with fire and the Sun in Indo-European tradition). Meadowsweet (*Filipendula ulmaria*, Mead Wort or Queen of the Meadow) was her sacred plant.

Anu or Ana

A great Land Goddess sometimes equated with Danu/Dana, she was the Divine Mother who nurtured the land. Landscape features such as hills were said to be her body. The Paps of Anu in Ireland are one example.

The Cailleach (Divine Hag or Old Woman)

Cailleachs existed over many Celtic areas, each associated with the land of a given locality. These were the ancient Land Goddess in her Hag form. As an old woman of great power and wisdom, she was associated with wells and hills and was said to travel with the deer herds while riding on the back of a wolf. The only creation story we have from Celtic lore says that she created the islands of Britain by dropping stones "from her apron" (vagina) and by wielding a mighty hammer to create and shape the land, raising mountains and crafting valleys and rivers. In Scottish lore she was the great Crone of Winter, the other face of Brighid or Bride, who came to power in the dark and cold half of the year. She turned to stone at Beltaine (May Day) when her alter ego, Bride, washed her face in the Well of Youth and was reborn as the Divine Hag at Samhain (All Hallows Eve).

The modern negative connotations of the word *hag* do not correlate to how this term was viewed in ancient Celtic culture. *Hag* is related to the Greek *hagios* meaning "saintly" or "holy" and the Old English *hægtesse* meaning "a woman of prophetic and oracular powers". So, *hag* was a term that carried power and respect.

Elen

Also known as Elen of the Ways and the Deer Mother, Elen is sometimes pictured as the Green Woman, an antlered Goddess wearing green leaves with a dog at her side. The name *Elen* is related to ancient words for "deer" and "reindeer" (*severen elen* is reindeer in Bulgarian, and *elen* means "deer" in Macedonian, for example). It is an old female reindeer that always leads the herd. The nurturing, Creatrix Deer Mother was revered as the source of life, death, and rebirth by those who lived closely with the reindeer. Reindeer once frequented the northern Celtic lands.

Epona

A Gaulish and Celt-Iberian fertility Goddess who was associated with horses and was eventually adopted as a Goddess by the ancient Roman cavalry, Epona appears as a young woman seated on a horse, often with a colt at her side. At times she is depicted with a sheaf of wheat in her lap, grasping a serpent in her left hand, and holding a dish of grain in her right hand. One Gaulish tile shows her riding a reined goose (could

Figure 9. Epona flanked by two horses, sitting on a throne, holding a fruit basket on her lap.

This relief is from Köngen, Germany, circa 200 CE and is housed at the Historic Museum of Bern. Photo by Xuan Che, CC BY 2.0/Wikimedia Commons.

she be the original Mother Goose?). She was the Divine Protectress of Horses and a Sovereignty Goddess.

Flidais, Flidas, Fliodhas, or Fliodhais

Held by some to be an Artemis-like Deer Goddess, Flidais was also a Goddess of cows and of fertility. When she was away from her husband, Fergus, he needed seven ordinary women just to satisfy him. She possessed a magical herd of cows that gave enough milk for an army every seven days, and a white cow that could feed three hundred men from one night's milking. Her son milked wild deer as if they were cows, by the powers received from his mother.

Modron (Great Mother)

A Welsh Land Goddess and Great Mother Goddess, she was the Primal Being who always was and always will be. Her son was called Maponos or Mabon (Divine Youth). His full title was Mabon vab Modron (Son of Mother), and he had no father. Incidentally, Mabon is not connected in any way to the Fall Equinox. That idea was invented by Pagan author Aidan Kelly in the 1970s.

Sheelagh-Na-Gig

A figure of immense power; the image of Sheelagh-Na-Gig was placed on buildings and walls to avert the evil eye. She was a fertility and

Figure 10. A twelth-century Sheelagh-Na-Gig.
This statue is on the church at Kilpeck, Herefordshire, England. CC BY-SA 3.0/Wikimedia Commons.

healing Goddess in her Cailleach (Divine Hag, Old Woman) form who was carved with a prominent, open vulva. Her exaggerated genitals symbolize the cycles of birth, death, and regeneration. Touching her vulva or rubbing dust from it was said to bring regeneration, fertility, and healing. Christian churches made use of the veneration of this figure and placed her carved likeness over doorways (perhaps to lure in Pagans?).

Tailtiu

The Great Land Goddess who was the foster mother of the God Lugh. He created the festival of Lughnasad as funeral games in her honor. It is said that Lugh will cause destructive storms to arise if his foster mother is not honored at Lughnasad.

Tlachtga

From *tlacht* (earth) and *gae* (spear), her name may mean Thunderbolt Woman. She was a Land Goddess and also patroness of the Druids. The fire of Tlachtga was lit on the Hill of Ward, near Athboy, County Meath, the site of a yearly Samhain Druidic assembly during the reign of Tuthal Teachmair (d. around 100 CE).

Goddesses of Rivers, Springs, and Wells

Water is another sacred aspect of creation without which we cannot survive. The Goddesses associated with water bring us life, health, cleansing, and beauty.

Arnemetia

The name of the Goddess of the sacred spring at Buxton, England, means, "she who dwells over the sacred grove." Other Goddesses who are Spirits within the sacred Grove are Nemetona, Goddess of the Nemeton, or sacred space, and Belissama, a Gaulish Goddess. Depictions of Leucetius and Nemetona, a divine couple, were found at Aquae Sulis, in Bath, England, and in northeastern Gaul.

Boann or Board

Her name means, "she of the white cattle." She was the Irish Sacred Mother River Goddess of the River Boyne and of the Milky Way, the mother of Brighid, and the wife of the Water God, Nechtan. A Cow Goddess of great wisdom, her imagery derives from Vedic sources where sacred rivers of milk flow from a mystical cow. In Irish tradition a person who drinks from the river Boyne in June will become a seer-poet.

Brigantia

The High One, Brigantia, was a Goddess of high places and of the hearth and sacred fire. A British name for the Goddess Brighid who was associated with sacred wells and streams, she was the Sacred Mother River Goddess of the rivers Braint and Brent, and the tutelary Goddess of the Brigantes (Yorkshire area). She was also a pastoral Goddess who was guardian of the cattle and other herd animals. In Romano-Celtic Britain she was equated with the Roman Goddess Caelestis and thus became known as Caelestis-Brigantia.

Broenela

A Celt-Iberian Goddess of bread, fermentation, and fertility whose name may derive from *broa* (corn/wheat bread). She may also be an aquatic Goddess and a Goddess of Storms.

The Cailleach (Divine Hag or Old Woman)

The Ancient Veiled One and Crone Goddess who was associated with sacred wells in Irish and British areas. She was the creatrix of rivers, hills, and other landscape features. (See also the Cailleach on page 39 and Sheelagh-Na-Gig on page 41.)

Clota

The Sacred Mother River Goddess of the River Clyde.

Coventina

A triple Goddess of springs and wells. (See page 36 for more on Coventina.)

Dea Matrona

Sacred Mother River Goddess of the source of the Marne River.

Latis

A British Goddess of the Pool and the Goddess of Beer. An appropriate Goddess for brewers and mead-makers to propitiate.

Nabia

A Celt-Iberian Goddess associated with wild, forested places, river valleys, mountain sanctuaries, and sacred springs. She was a popular Goddess of water, sky, earth, health, fertility, and wealth. Her name may derive from *nawa* or *nava* (water courses). Her epithets include Lady of the Vale, She who lives in the Valley, and Winding River.

Sequana

The Sacred Mother River Goddess of the Seine River and the source of the Seine in Gaul. She was depicted as traveling in a duck-prowed vessel,

Figure 11. Bronze statue of the Gallo-Roman goddess Sequana.
This statue is housed in the archaeological museum in Dijon, France. Public domain.

wearing a diadem, and holding her arms open to welcome pilgrims who came to her shrine seeking healing.

Shannon or Siannon

The Sacred Mother River Goddess of the river Shannon.

Sulis or Sulis-Minerva

The Romans compared Sulis, associated with the Sun and with healing wells and springs, to Minerva. The great Aquae Sulis healing springs in Bath, England, were dedicated to her. Her name comes from the Celtic *suli* (eye) and the proto-Celtic root sūli-, related to the various Indo-European words for "sun". In Sulis we have a Solar Goddess whose presence at healing springs and baths brings about the classic Indo-European combination of fire and water, the two basic building blocks of creation. Where fire and water come together there is the greatest potential for magic and transformation.

Tamesis

The Sacred Mother River Goddess of the Thames River.

Figure 12. Bronze head of the statue of Sulis-Minerva.

This head was found on Stall Street in Bath in 1727 and is housed at the Roman Baths Museum. Photo by Ad Meskens, CC BY-SA 3.0/Wikimedia Commons.

Trebaruna

A Celt-Iberian Goddess linked to flowing water and springs in mountainous areas. Her name may come from *treba* (house) and *runa* (secret)—marking her as a domestic Goddess or Spirit of the Home. Or her name may derive from *arunis* (movement, river). She was both a tribal Goddess and an aquatic Goddess and possibly Goddess of the Village Fountain. It is worth remembering that in ancient times a fountain of clean water was a source of health and also the basis for women's work such as cooking and laundry.

Verbeia

The Sacred Mother Goddess of the river Wharfe who was shown holding serpents.

Goddesses of Battle and the Hunt

Goddesses (and women!) were not seen by the Celts as passive, meek individuals. Every Goddess was assumed to be a fertile love Goddess, and at the same time many Goddesses were also experts in the arts of hunting and of war.

Badb Catha

Battle Crow, an Irish War Goddess who was part of the holy trinity of the Morrígan (with Macha and Nemain). She influenced the outcome of battles and once helped the Tuatha Dé Danann gain victory over the Fomorians at the Battle of Magh Tuireadh (Moytura). She was cognate with the Gaulish Goddess Cathbodua, also Battle Crow, who was a Goddess of war and of ravens.

Madb

Mabd, from *mead*, was known as She Who Intoxicates or Drunk Woman. A Mother-Warrior Goddess of sex and strong drink who could run faster than the swiftest horse. The mere sight of her robbed a man of two-thirds of his strength, and she was so skilled as a warrior that she used physical weapons rather than magic to win her battles. She had many sexual partners and discarded them at will—in fact, she required sex with three different men a day! She was also the mother of many children.

Macha

A powerful Battle Goddess who appeared dressed in red. She carried a mirror in her hand with a maze pictured on it, symbolic of her role in taking souls beyond this life. She was another aspect of the Morrígan (see page 38).

Goddesses of Magic, Healing, and the Otherworld

Celtic Goddesses were mistresses of many arts. Druids, nobles, and the common people looked to these Goddesses for aid and inspiration. Develop a relationship with them and watch your own skills blossom!

Airmid

Patroness of herbalists, she was the daughter of Dian Cécht a physician of the Tuatha Dé Danann. She and her father guarded a healing well that brought the dead back to life. Dian Cécht once created a silver hand for King Nuada because no king could rule if he was blemished, and the king had lost a hand. Airmid's brother Miach restored the severed hand of the king further by replacing it with a fully functional live one. This feat made Dian Cécht so jealous that he killed Miach in a fit of rage. When Miach was buried, three hundred and sixty-five healing herbs emerged from his body, indicating by their position the parts of the human body they would cure (and possibly a now-lost calendrical system). Airmid picked the herbs and arranged them on her cloak in their correct positions but, Dian Cécht, ever jealous, scattered the herbs so that humanity would lose the knowledge of their virtues. The Goddess Airmid now reveals the secret uses of these plants to her devotees.

Arentio and Arentia

A Celt-Iberian divine couple associated with private family worship, fertility, and the health and protection of public and private spaces. There are nine known ancient altars dedicated to Arentio and/or Arentia, all in the Portuguese inner Beira and Spanish Extremadura. On one altar dedicated to Arentia is the name Equotullaicensi, implying a connection to horses.

Arianrhod

The daughter and/or wife of Don, she was a Welsh Goddess of the Moon and of the Milky Way. Her name meant "silver wheel" or "silver circle." She was the Mistress of Fate and weaver of the silver threads of life. Her home was called Caer Arianrhod (the Fort of the Silver Wheel, or the Milky Way), which was seen as a place of death, rebirth, and initiation.

Carman

A Goddess of magic who used spells, charms, and incantations to destroy her enemies. She had three sons named Dian (Violent), Dubh (Black), and Dothur (Evil) who excelled at violence, dishonesty, and theft. The Sons of Carman wanted to conquer Ireland and destroy the Tuatha Dé Danann, so they blighted all the wheat in the land. But the Tuatha Dé Danann had better magic; they sang spells and satires upon the Sons of Carman, driving them into the sea. They also kept Carman as a hostage until her death. She died of longing for her lost sons and was buried in Wexford among the Oak trees. After that, her grave was honored with a yearly festival at Lughnasad.

Cerridwen

A Sorceress who possessed a magical Cauldron of Transformation. She was a muse of inspiration and initiation who hastened the mystical progress of her devotees.

Clidna or Cliodhna

An Irish Goddess of great beauty known as the Fairy Queen of Carraig Cliodhna in County Cork. She was associated with the Summerland of Bliss where feasting and horse racing go on continuously, and there is no death, decay, or violence. She has three brightly colored birds who eat apples from an Otherworldly tree and whose sweet song heals the sick.

Rhiannon or Rigantona

A British Goddess who was said to ride a magic horse. She appeared to be moving at a slow and stately pace, yet no mortal horse could overtake her (possibly a reference to the Moon—no matter how fast you travel on a horse you can never catch up to it!). Her name means "great queen," and she was often associated with birds.

Goddess of the Sun and Moon

As Druids we spend as much time as we can in nature, under the Sun, Moon, and stars. As we feel the Sun's rays on our skin, or bask in the light of the Moon, we acknowledge their divine feminine energy.

Grian

Grian is an Old Irish word for the Sun. In Celtic thinking (and in Baltic and Germanic thought as well), both the Sun and Moon were regarded as female. The Sun and Moon were said to be sisters, and the Moon was once brighter than the Sun but became obscured by her jealous sibling. Grian, a pre-Christian Sun Goddess, was associated with County Limerick and Cnoc Greine (Hill of Grian, Hill of the Sun). There was an old Irish tradition of two Suns: Áine representing the light half of the year and the bright summer Sun (*an ghrian mhór*) and Grian as the Goddess of Winter representing the dark half of the year and the pale winter Sun (*an ghrian bheag*). Tober Cil-na-Greina (the well of the fountain of the Sun) is in County Cork.

In *Ancient Legends, Mystic Charms & Superstitions of Ireland*, Lady Jane Francesca Agnes Wilde (1821–1896) wrote of the Tober Cil-na-Greina:

The ritual observed was very strict at the beginning three draughts of water were taken by the pilgrims, the number of drinks three, the number of rounds on their knees were three, thus making the circuit of the well nine times. After each round the pilgrim laid a stone on the ancient altar in the Druid circle called "the well of the sun," and these stones, named in Irish "the stones of the sun," are generally pure white, and about the size of a pigeon's egg. They have a beautiful appearance after rain when the sun shines on them, and were doubtless held sacred to the sun in pagan times.[1]

The Gods

When we contemplate nature, we see that there are both masculine and feminine energies in plants, animals, and people. Also, along with the great Goddesses, there are masculine counterparts and consorts who bestow their uniquely male sacred gifts. Celtic women and men sought to grow closer to these divine masculine energies, to empower and enliven their lives and spiritual journeys. As with Celtic Goddesses, each God was assumed to be intelligent, fertile, and sexy, no matter his special sphere or function.

Horned Gods

The Horned Gods come down to us from Neolithic, proto-Celtic, and Bronze Age times. Their antlers may represent the waxing and waning of yearly agricultural and nature cycles because antlers, like the vegetation, bud in the spring, grow full in the summer, and drop off in winter. Celtic statues have been found with removable horns, which to me implies that the antlers were set aside at certain feasts, or at certain times of the year, possibly in sync with the wild horned animals and/or the winter disappearance and then reappearance of greenery.

Some Horned Gods are associated with water and are depicted holding an anchor or in and around ships. The serpent, bull, and ram are also connected to the Horned God. Occasionally he wears bull horns and or appears with a ram-headed serpent.

In general, stags and stag attributes like antlers represent wild hunted creatures, while bulls and bull horns denote domestic beasts and wealth. Rams and ram horns express warrior qualities. Horns may also have a phallic significance or be connected to the cornucopia, a hollow, horn-shaped vessel from which riches flow.

Caerno

A Celt-Iberian God of hard, rocky places, boulders, and cairns. God of the flocks and of shepherds.

Cernunnos

Known today as the archetypal Horned God, we assume his name from a single inscription on a single relief in Paris, France: *ernunnos*. Other Horned Ones are known from rock art such as at Valcamonica in Northern Italy, where he is shown wearing a long robe and bearing antlers. Similar figures are found in Spain, Germany, Denmark, Ireland, and Britain.

There is a Cernunnos-type antlered figure, or Horned God, on the Gundestrup Cauldron, where he appears as Lord of the Animals, sitting in a half-lotus position surrounded by various beasts (see figure 2 on page 24). He is wearing a torc, symbolic of his noble status, and is grasping a ram-horned serpent in one hand and a torc in the other.

Cernunnos is sometimes shown feeding sacred serpents from a dish or with a serpent coiling around his waist. He may also be associated with coins or with a cornucopia filled with grapes, symbolic of his role as patron of commerce. Wealth was counted in cattle by the ancient Celts, and a cow horn or cornucopia was an obvious symbol of riches (ram horns were connected to warriors).

Sylvanus or Silvanus

An antlered God of the Forest, he was associated with the hunt and with the Spirit of wild places. A Divine Hunter who was often depicted naked.

Gods of War and Battle

Through a kind of guild system, people once worshipped Goddesses and Gods of the same skill set. As one example, the warriors of a tribe would turn to Gods of Battle for inspiration and strength in times of conflict.

Belatucadros

Fair Shining One, or Fair Slayer, was a God of War from Northern Britain who was once worshipped by foot soldiers. The Romans equated him with Mars.

Braciaca

Braciaca's name, Drunk on Malt, may be derived from the Welsh word for malt (*brag/brac*). Possibly a God of malt-induced intoxication. Alcohol was once given to warriors as they set off for battle, and Braciaca was equated with Mars by the Romans.

Camulos

This God was also associated with Mars by the Romans. He was depicted wearing an Oak coronet. He was worshipped in both Gaul and Britain and was the local God of Camulodunum (Fort of Camulos) now known as Colchester.

Cocidius

Otherwise known as the Red One, the Horned God of North Britain, the root of his name may be the Welsh word *coch* (red). Rudiobus was another Gaulish warrior God associated with the color red, and In Ruad Rofhessa—the Red One of Great Knowledge—is the one title of the Dagda. The Romans associated warriors and the God Mars with the color red.

Sacred Warrior Protector Gods

In common with Native Americans and other Indigenous, tribal peoples, the Celts expected their warrior Gods to be intelligent healers, providers, and protectors of the people. These attributes are often found in the warrior deities the Celts admired.

Every tribe once had its own Sacred Warrior Protector God. When Christianity took over and the people were told to put their faith elsewhere, the strong folk memory of a Divine Protector God persisted. For example, in modern times all British peoples seem to have conflated their hopes into one legendary individual: King Arthur, the Once and Future King. Instead of a local tribal protector deity, their common expectations are pinned on one lone overarching figure who, it is said, will reappear when their need is greatest.

Alator

A British warrior God whose name may mean "he who rears or nourishes his people," Alator is an example of the sacred warrior as nourisher of the tribe.

Artos (Arthur)

The Bear was most likely a fifth-century king and battle leader. He has now taken on the classic functions of the tribal sacred warrior protector deity of the Celtic peoples. He is tied to the Cauldron of Transformation and Regeneration via the mystery of the grail (the grail is just a smaller version of the magical Celtic cauldron). As a child, Arthur was taught the speech of the animals by the Druid Merlin, linking him with Cernunnos in his Lord of the Animals aspect. Many of the warriors surrounding Arthur had supernatural healing abilities, another hallmark of the sacred warrior protector God. It appears that the British Celtic people, deprived of their tribal sacred warrior protector Gods by the new religion of Christianity, chose this figure to invest with the ancient tradition of the Divine King and Savior who protects the tribe.

Bandua, Bandu, or Bandia

He or She of Victory and He or She of the Horses or Chariot. A Celt-Iberian Goddess or God (or divine pair?). A protector deity of the local community, of fortified settlements and of war. A deity (or deities?) that brings fortune, prosperity, and protection to the people. On one *patera* (dish) the deity is portrayed as a female figure holding a cornucopia, surrounded by four altars and a tree, resembling the Roman Goddess Fortuna.

Condatis

British God of where the waters meet. Condatis was associated with healing waters, sacred springs, and war. He was once venerated by the lower classes.

Dagda or An Daghda

The Irish Good God was both a warrior God and patron of the Druids. He had a magical staff that dealt death at one end and restored life with the other. As a sacred warrior protector of the tribes, he had a great, inexhaustible Cauldron of Plenty from which he fed the people. The ever-full cauldron was one of the treasures of the Tuatha Dé Danann. He was an example of the warrior as intelligent magician, wiseman, provider, and healer. An Daghda mated with the Morrígan and with the Goddess Boann and was the father of many illustrious progeny: Aed, Angus Óg, Bodb Dearg, Brighid, Danu, Cermait, Ogma, Ainge, Midhir, Nuadu, Dian Cécht, Eiriu, Banba, and Fodla. He lived at Brú na Bóinne (Newgrange in County Meath) until he handed it over to his son, Angus Óg. He bore the titles Samildánach (many skilled) and Aedh (fire), a fitting name for the father of the great Fire Goddess, Brighid. He possessed a magical harp that when played, set the seasons into their correct order.

Durbedico

A Celt-Iberian aquatic God whose name may mean "dripper." Possibly the God of the river Ave or of fountains.

Loucetius or Leucetius

This God is known as the Bright One or Shining One and is possibly another incarnation of Lugh. He is paired with Nemetona, the Goddess of the Sacred Grove, in a depiction at the healing springs of Bath (Aquae Sulis). Loucetius was a horned warrior God who was also a healer; he was a classic tribal warrior protector deity.

Lugh

Known in Ireland as Lugh Samildánach (Lugh from proto-Indo-European *lewgh* meaning "to bind by oath," and "the many skilled") and Lugh Lámfada, Lugh of the Long Hand, a reference to the Gae Assail, his magical spear, one of the four treasures of the Tuatha Dé Danann. He was Master of Every Art and the patron God of the Lughnasad festival, which he created in honor of his foster mother Tailtiu. Lugh had several magical possessions including his fiery spear that never missed its mark, a sword called Freagarach (Answerer) that could pierce any armor, a sling stone, a boat named Wave-Sweeper, which obeyed the thoughts of the person riding in it and needed no sails or oars, a magical hound named Failinis, and a horse that could travel on land or sea.

Figure 13. A three-headed Lugh.
This was discovered in 1852 in Reims.
Photo by QuartierLatin1968, CC BY-SA 3.0/
Wikimedia Commons.

Lugh is said to have invented *fidchell* (Welsh *gwyddbwyll*, the equivalent of chess), ball games, and horse racing, and was so brilliant at strategy that he often used magic to defeat his enemies, rather than brute force and weapons. He was the most universally admired pan-Celtic deity, known as the pan-Celtic Lugus, and the Welsh Lleu Llaw Gyffes. He was equated with Mercury, as well as Apollo. He is the father of Cuchulainn, the most famous warrior in the North of Ireland.

In the Christian era Saint Michael took on many of Lugh's attributes as both a sacred warrior protector and patron of the harvest. Both Lugh and Michael are said to confront and defeat the forces of destructive power such as thunderstorms and blight, which could harm the crops. The ancient Celts preferred high places with a good view of the country-side for their rites sacred to Lugh. Christians would often rededicate such hilltop sites to Saint Michael and built churches dedicated to Michael right on top of the old sacred sites of Lugh. Mont St. Michel in France and the Michael Mount in Cornwall are two such examples.

In Celt-Iberian areas he was known as Lugus, a God of Skill and of shoemakers (among other crafts). In sculptures he was shown with a triple face (triplicity is always a sign of a high God or Goddess in Indo-European thinking). Lugus was a God who transcended specific functions and forms—in epigraphic evidence his name is plural. The Matronae, or Triple Mothers, were worshipped in the same places as the Triple Lugus.

Nemetius
Whose name means "sacred one," was a sacred warrior God worshipped on the west bank of the Rhine River.

Nodons or Nodens
A British warrior God known as He Who Bestows Wealth and Cloud Maker. He was the River God of the Severn Estuary. A God of healing through Sun and water, he was associated both with hunting and with dogs. In Celtic thinking dogs were symbolic of healing and small figu-

rines of dogs have been found as offerings in British healing shrines (it's quite possible that the Celts used dogs to lick wounds or to restore circulation to injured limbs). We know that there was once a sanctuary of the Greek God of Medicine Asklepios (Roman Aesculapius), where part of the healing treatment or ritual was to receive licks from a sacred dog.

Nuadu or Nuada Airgetlamh

Nuada of the Silver Hand is the Irish equivalent of Nodens. His magical sword was one of the four treasures of the Tuatha Dé Danann and once it was unsheathed, no one could escape from it. Nuada lost a hand in battle, and since the Celts had a rule that a king must be without blemish, had a new hand made that functioned just like a flesh and blood appendage (see Airmid, above).

Reue

A widely worshipped Celt-Iberian God of sovereignty associated with mountains, rivers, or river valleys. His name may be derived from *hreu* (river, water stream) or *rewe* (field, plain). As bringers of prosperity, health, and sovereignty, bulls were sacrificed to him, denoting his high status. Reue was possibly the celestial mountain God who fed the mountain springs and rivers.

Rigisamus

His name means "most kingly," and the Romans also equated this warrior God of Gaul and Britain with Mars. He was an example of the sacred warrior as a noble, kingly leader.

Toutates

Toutates was the God of the People (from *touta*, "the people"). This Gaulish warrior God and tribal deity led his people in both war and peace and showed them how to win wealth through the spoils of battle. To the Romans, he also became Mars. (See how he was involved with the marriage of Esus on pages 60 to 61.)

Gods of Divine Skill

Persons of art, such as physicians, smiths, and poets would turn to Gods of Skill to empower and inspire their own creative efforts since, in Celtic thinking, the object was to become just like one's chosen deity, hopefully emulating them in brilliance and achievement.

Dian Cécht

A God of physicians whose talents were eclipsed by those of his son Miach (see Airmid above). In a fit of jealous rage Dian Cécht wounded his son several times and finally killed him. Dian Cécht's daughter, Airmid, discovered herbs growing on Miach's grave that would cure every human ill. She carefully arranged them on her cloak, showing by their positions which part of the body they would heal. But Dian Cécht deliberately kicked the cloak, scattering the herbs and depriving humanity of their benefits. To me this sounds an awful lot like the struggles between the beliefs of allopathic medical doctors and traditional herbalists!

Endouellicus or Endovelicus

A God of healing, prophecy, and the Underworld, associated with vegetation and the afterlife, he was accepted by the Romans who conflated him with Pluto or to Serapis. A Celt-Iberian deity whose name may come from *bel* or *vel*, Phoenician for "lord." His name may also come from the Celtic *vailos*, meaning "wolf", because wolves were his symbolic animals. He had a temple where oracles and visions were sought, similar to the Temple of Apollo at Delphi where steam issued from the ground, inducing prophetic trance.

Goibniu or Govannon

A divine smith who fashioned magical Otherworldly weapons for the Gods. According to tradition, Goibniu, Credne, and Luchtainel, known as the Trí Dée Dána (the Three Gods of Art), made the weapons used by the Tuatha Dé Danann to defeat the Fomorians.

Lugh

Lugh Samildánach (Lugh from proto-Indo-European *lewgh* meaning "to bind by oath," and "the many skilled") was Master of Every Art (see above) and patron of the Lughnasad festival in August. (See also the entry for Lugh on page 55).

Oghma

Inventor of the pre-Latin Ogham alphabet and possibly the same God as the Gallic God Ogmios, his name comes from the Indo-European root *ak-* or *ag-* meaning "to cut," referring to the method in which Ogham was incised into stone and wood. Also known as Sun Faced (Grianainech) and Strongman (Trenfher), he was a God of eloquent speech. It was said that his bardic followers were bound to him by a golden chain that was attached to his tongue.

Gods of Magic and the Elements

As denizens of the Otherworld, the Gods of Magic have a powerful influence over this world too. They are able to cross the veil and affect the course of the seasons, nature, and people's lives.

Angus Óg

Young Angus was a son of the Dagda by Boann (Goddess of the river Boyne). He was a God of Love and the patron of young people and young lovers whom he assisted in their affairs. He played a golden harp and was a resident deity of Brú na Bóinne (the Palace of the Boyne) now called Newgrange, in County Meath, Ireland.

Belenos or Belinus

Shining or Fair Shining One, he was a Gaulish Sun Deity associated with the Beltaine festival. He was the patron of sheep and cattle.

Esus

A Gaulish Earth God of trees and of everything that grows from the soil, this chthonic guardian of nature and of plants lived under the

Figure 14. Esus on the Pillar of Boatman.
Housed in the Musée de Cluny-Musée National du Moyen Âge.
CC BY-SA 3.0/Wikimedia Commons.

earth and protected everything growing out of it. Esus and Taranis (see below) shared a common wife, the Goddess Rigani. Esus stole Rigani away from Taranis and brought her to the Underworld where he married her. When Taranis became enraged over this, the God Teutates had to shield both Esus and Rigani from Taranis's wrath. This seems to be a tale that accounts for the changing of the seasons when the power of the land stays above ground in the light half the year, and below ground in the dark half of the year (the Celts only recognized two seasons; summer and winter).

Manannán MacLir or Manawydan Ap Llyr

Possessor of the crane bag of many powers (see page 114) he had a magical cloak with the power of *fith-fath,* an invisibility and shape-changing spell. Manannán was associated with liminal spaces between the water and the land, symbolic of his ability to travel from one world to the next, from life to death and back. He is a God of the Sea who rides over the oceans in his chariot and herds the fish as his flocks.

Taranis

Taranis, the Thunderer, was a Gaulish God whose symbol was the sacred wheel. He was associated with lightning and with Oak trees, trees that attract lightning and yet survive the blast. The Romans equated him with Jupiter and the Scandinavians compared him to Thor and all deities connected to storms, lightning, Oak trees, and high places. As a Sky God who rules the weather, Taranis rolls his sacred wheel across the heavens, which causes rain and thunder to manifest.

Ancestor Gods

Ancestor worship is a strong element of Celtic religion and thought. The Otherworld is not in some faraway place: the Spirits of the ancestors are said to mix freely with the living and be particularly accessible at the fire festivals of Beltaine (May Day) and Samhain (Halloween). Powerful Gods rule the Ancestor's realm, which is under the ground. Offerings to the ancestors and to the Ancestor Gods are dropped into water or into pits dug into the earth or simply laid on the soil.

Dis Pater

A Gaulish God of wealth, the Underworld, and fertility, he was the primal Ancestor God of the Gauls who may have been another aspect of Cernunnos. The Romans admired this God so much that they built a sanctuary for him in Rome that became the cave where the Roman state treasures were held.

Donn

The Ancestor God of the Milesian Celts who came from Northern Spain (Galicia) and settled in Ireland. Tech Duinn (the House of Donn) is an Irish name for the Otherworld, specifically as the realm of the dead, and Donn was the ruler of the dead. Tech Duinn is often identified with Baoi Bhéarra (or Oileán Baoi), a rocky islet near Dursey Island at the extreme southwestern end of the Beara peninsula, County Cork.

The following sources were invaluable references for the descriptions of the Goddesses and Gods throughout this chapter: the blog *Golden Trail: A Wayfarer's Path*, particularly the "Bandua" post; Penny Hill's article "Healing Power of Dogs"; Mary Jones's Celtic Encyclopedia website, particularly "Oghma Grianainech"; Juan Carlos Olivares Pedreño's article "Celtic Gods of the Iberian Peninsula"; Anne Ross's book *Pagan Celtic Britain*; and Lady Jane Francesca Agnes Wilde's book *Ancient Legends, Mystic Charms & Superstitions of Ireland*.

The Druidic Festivals and High Holy Days

Three things to be seriously considered every day: the laws of love and kindliness, the duty of hospitality, and the service of the Gods.

ANCIENT IRISH TRIAD

I ran Druid Groves here in the forest where I live for several decades. For twenty years and more people came once a month to camp and to learn Druidism. Our activities included reading books together and discussing them, taking walks in the woods, making offerings to a local river, playing music in the forest for the benefit of the Fairies (they loved it, especially the live harp music), doing rituals, and opening portals in the landscape to reach the Fairy Realms.

Druid Groves and solitary Druids met here for a Lughnasad camp every year for thirty years. The Lughnasad festival is a traditional time for gatherings and *oenachs* (fairs). As there are few Druids in the Pagan world as compared to Witches and Wiccans, to get a good group you usually have to pull in people from several states. We finally decided that August was the best time for folks to travel and camp out.

When we did open a portal, we would wait for some creature to show up, because that was our confirmation that the process had really worked. And something always appeared.

Once we were sitting in a circle under a large Oak tree and a huge yellow-and-black spider slowly let itself down to the exact center of our gathering and just hung there, watching us. Another time a moose showed up and for several days it graced the stone circle behind the house. A giant dragonfly landed on one of us at another gathering, and I will never forget the time a reporter came to interview us, and a flood of tiny green spiders appeared out of nowhere, dancing at our feet.

Running a Druid weekend can be hard work for the host because you have to stay on top of everything that is happening. Is there enough food, and if not, who will drive to the Stop and Shop to pick up something? Is there enough firewood and who will carry the logs to the ritual area and then competently lay out the fire? Did the fire tender remember to bring matches and are they dry? Did everyone bring adequate offerings for the fire altar, the sacred well, and the trees? Who will be taking which part in the ritual, and do they know the songs? Are they confident enough to say their lines? Did all participants contribute toward the porta potty? Did everyone find a good place to pitch their tent where they won't get washed out in a storm or have their tent burned down when someone cooks on the cooking fire nearby?

These and lots of other details mean that the host can never fully relax. After thirty years or so I found myself gradually losing my enthusiasm. Maybe it's the prerogative of getting older, but now my Druid activities are mostly online. I find myself happily circling with local Witches (bless them) who carry on the work of the live yearly round of festivals, and I don't even have to do the dishes (unless I want to!).

High Holy Days: Sacred Fire

The four great Druidic fire festivals are Samhain, Imbolc, Beltaine, and Lughnasad. They all feature sacred fire such as candles (at Imbolc) and/

or bonfires. These are a type of fire altar at the observances—prayers and offerings to Goddesses and Gods are given to the flames, which carry them upward to the Sky Realm of the deities.

Constructing a Need Fire

At times when there is a serious calamity in the community, Druids may undertake to create a very special type of fire altar called a *tein-eigin*, or need-fire.

Traditionally the need-fire was lit through friction and then became the source for bonfires with which healing magic for the community was performed at the fire festivals or when the community had a strong need, as for example the outbreak of a cattle disease or a pandemic. The need-fire was ritually prepared by married men who had removed all metal, including jewelry from their bodies. They drilled a stick into a dry piece of wood and fuel such as straw and bits of fungi found on Birch trees were added slowly as the friction from turning the stick began to create sparks. The wood was either entirely Oak or a combination of different woods considered sacred:

> *Choose the Willow of the streams,*
> *Choose the Hazel of the rocks,*
> *Choose the Alder of the marshes,*
> *Choose the Birch of the waterfalls,*
> *Choose the Ash of the shade,*
> *Choose the Yew of resilience,*
> *Choose the Elm of the brae,*
> *Choose the Oak of the Sun.*[1]

Additionally Apple or Pine may have been used.

If the attempts to start the fire weren't successful, there were questions for the community: Was one of the men assigned to fire-lighting concealing something? Was there a problem with the hearth-fire of someone in the community? When the affliction being addressed was severe, nine times nine (eighty-one) men were asked to build a large fire, from which all houses in the community rebuilt their hearth fires. Next, water from a sacred spring or Holy Well was boiled on the new fire (this had to be the first thing heated on the new fire). That water was then sprinkled on afflicted persons or animals.

Samhain

For Celtic Druids the year proper begins at Samhain. October 31–November 3 is the usual time for the modern observance. There are also those who place the Holy Day astronomically, at the exact mid-point between Fall Equinox and Winter Solstice. And an old date for Samhain was November 11–12 (I like to think that some wise person knew that and it's why they chose November 11 for Armistice Day, or Veterans Day as it's known in the United States, a time to honor deceased veterans).

This festival marks the official end of the harvest when all produce must be safely brought in from the fields and stored, and anything left outside after that belongs to the Fairies. It is also the time when the cows are brought back down from the hills and settled into their winter enclosures. Anyone familiar with wild mountain areas such as Yellowstone will have noticed that wild animals like bison do the same thing—they descend from the peaks to winter in the valley.

Samhain marks the portal between the light half of the year and the dark half of the year. It is the beginning of winter and of the dark season when storytelling can begin and indoor crafts and activities take precedence. It makes sense that the year begins in the dark because all life on Earth begins in darkness. A seed in the black soil is the start of a new plant, a human baby or a baby animal grows in the dark of the womb. Physicists agree that there is more dark matter in the universe than light, and that even stars are hatched in the dark. For the ancient Celts the day began at sunset, as night fell. The dark was not something to be feared, it was the source and dream from which all creation took shape.

According to the ancient Romano-Gaulish Coligny Calendar (a second-century Celtic calendar found in 1897 in Coligny, France), the first month is labeled TRINOX[tion] SAMO[nii] SINDIV "three-nights of Samonios today," meaning that this Holy Day was a three-day observance. We have already seen the importance of the number three, as in the triple High Goddesses and Gods. This feast must have been the most solemn observance of the ritual calendar year.

In Irish tradition all household fires were extinguished when Oiche Shamhna (Samhain) arrived, making this the darkest night of the year. The fires were then relit, ushering in the new Sun cycle. Druids lit a huge bonfire on the Hill of Tlachtga (near Athboy, County Meath), and burning torches were carried from there to every kingdom and household during the night (just like the Olympic flame).

It is worth remembering that Ireland at this time was composed of many tiny kingdoms that were often at odds with each other, stealing each other's cows and women. The bearing of torches from the Druidic central fire altar at Tlachtga to all the kingdoms was a way of creating spiritual unity among the tribes.

The Hill of Tlachtga itself is named for a Druidess, the daughter of the Sorcerer and Druid Mug Ruith, who traveled and studied magic with her father. She died giving birth to triplets who were born on the hill. As we have seen, the reference to triplets (the number three again) marks her as a divine figure.

Tlachtga was also a fertility Goddess of the Luigni, an Erainn tribe. The Hill of Tlachtga, which is near Tara, was a center of Celtic religious worship over two thousand years ago. According to tradition Tlachtga is buried on the hill, and I have been told the Samhain fire at Tlachtga was lit by women in her honor. If so, this would be a nice balance to the ritual of the Beltaine fire at Uisneach (see page 74).

Samhain is the time to honor the ancestors and all who are in the Spirit world. Thanks are given to the beloved dead who fought, loved, and sacrificed so that we may have good lives today. Honor and respect are given to the Nature Spirits, plants, and animals who have gifted their lives and energy for our sustenance. And traditionally it is the time to finish the harvest, cull the herds and preserve the meat as green nature dies back and the Earth retreats into her winter slumber.

The walls between the worlds are very thin at this time and the ancestors, Fairies, and the dead more easily return to visit their old homes and haunts. With so many Spirits about, people dress up to disguise themselves as protection from malevolent forces and carve turnips or rutabagas lit with candles, to frighten away the wandering dead. Pumpkins are not Celtic. They are native to America!

The Goddess most associated with Samhain in the tales is the Morrígan, the triple Goddess of crows, ravens, and battle. She is said to have mated with the Dagda at Samhain while straddling the river Unius. Thus the terrifying and powerful Dark Goddess of Death and Battle unites with the wise, Sacred Warrior Protector God, ensuring the strength, fertility, and well-being of the tribes.

If you happen to live near the ocean, Samhain is a good time to make thanks offerings to the Sea God Seonaidh (pronounced Shownee). In parts of Scotland, even at the start of the Christian era, it was held that by doing this a good crop of seaweed, which is both edible and an important fertilizer for crops, could be expected.

Figure 15. A traditional Irish turnip Jack-o'-lantern from the early twentieth century.
Housed at the Museum of Country Life, Ireland. Photo by Rannṗáirtí Anaitnid, CC BY-SA 3.0/Wikimedia Commons.

The ceremony was done in the dark. Afterward everyone went to church, lit a candle, then put it out, and regathered to drink and have a party, long into the night. Shony could be a Scots-Irish rendition of "Johnny" (Ian and Sean or Shane are John, as in Saint John). But the act of offering a sacrifice to a Sea God would seem to have much deeper Pagan roots.

Imbolc

The next fire festival in our seasonal round is Imbolc (February 1–2 in modern Pagan practice) from Old Irish *imbolg* (in the belly), referring to pregnant ewes, or from the Old Irish *imb-fholc* (to cleanse or wash oneself), referring to a kind of ritual cleansing.[2]

There are different ways to calculate the date of this Holy Day. Some will just follow the calendar, while others wait until the local sheep begin giving milk. In my area this happens around mid-February.

Imbolc is in essence a milk festival, in celebration of the lactation of the ewes. In Celtic times there were no supermarkets, and for several months of the year there would have been no milk. Sheep began to give milk again a few days before they dropped their lambs, around the time of Imbolc, which was cause for a celebration. Imbolc was also a fire festival because at this time it became light enough that one no longer had to carry a candle to the barn to do the milking.

The combination of milk (sacred liquid) and candle flame (sacred fire) brings together the two basic building blocks of creation in Indo-European thinking: fire and water, and the greatest potential for magic. The Christian church took over the festival and renamed it Candle Mass (Candlemas) and congregants were instructed to bring their candles to the altar to be blessed.

In Ireland Imbolc is considered the start of spring and time for the first plowings. Imbolc is the season when snakes and hedgehogs are seen to emerge from their winter denning, an occurrence that has led directly to the American tradition of Groundhog Day. See this Scottish traditional, from the *Carmina Gadelica*:

Early on Bride's morn
The serpent shall come from the hole,
I will not molest the serpent,
Nor will the serpent molest me.[3]

As described previously, Imbolc is the festival sacred to the Goddess Brighid (*Bride* in Scotland), a Fire Goddess of healing, poetry, smithcraft, and motherhood (see page 35). She was so popular in Celtic areas that they could never quite let go of her and her stories eventually morphed into the personage of Saint Brighid of Kildare who kept a Fire Temple, just as her Pagan predecessors once did.

In Ireland it is customary to weave Brighid's crosses out of rushes at Imbolc, to be hidden in eaves and placed in windows to attract the saint's blessings. But these crosses are not the Latin cross (which has a longer stem and three shorter arms). They are an equal-armed, solar cross: a Celtic version of the swastika. *Swastika* comes from Sanskrit *svastika* (good fortune, or well-being). The solar cross may have first been used in Eurasia, as early as seven thousand years ago. It is a sacred symbol in Hinduism, Buddhism, Jainism, and Odinism and a common sight on temples and houses in India and Indonesia.[4] It's even a good luck symbol for the Navaho Nation.

Another custom is to make a Brighid's girdle, a circle of rope with

Figure 16. Bride's cross, also known as Brigid's cross or Brighid's cross, these are usually woven of rushes, wheat stalks or similar. They can be Christian or Pagan symbols, depending on context.
Image shared by Culnacreann, CC BY-SA 3.0/Wikimedia Commons.

Figure 17. Swastikas on ancient Greek pottery.
From a collection at the Archaeological Museum of Thebes. Public domain.

Figure 18. Coin with Pegasos, with curved wing, flying on one side and incise
in the form of a swastika on the other.
*From Corinth circa 550–500 BCE. Image shared
by Exekias, CC BY 2.0/Wikimedia Commons.*

three Brighid's crosses tied to it. Women gracefully lower the circle over their heads to their feet to assume the protection of the Goddess or perhaps to be symbolically reborn from her womb, while men step through the "girdle."

Another custom is described by English professor Joe Pellegrino in "St. Brigid's Crosses and Girdles":

On the eve of St. Brigid's Feast (February 1, the Celtic feast of Imbolc, for renewal and purification) traditionally, young boys called *brideoga* or *biddies* would carry a churndash (the post used for churning butter) dressed as a woman, with an effigy of St. Brigid, and ask door to door for gifts or alms. O Cathasaigh notes that the churndash is symbolic of milking which has relevance both to the saint, who attended to a dairy, and to the festival of Imbolc. In addition to begging for alms, the brideoga would leave bundles of straw and rushes outside the doors at homes. At nightfall young girls would pick them up, and, after asking to be admitted in the name of the saint, would weave them into crosses. After traditional prayers and a meal, crosses would then be placed under the eaves in the house or in outhouses. Before they were placed in the thatch, however, the crosses would sometimes be blessed with holy water, a ritual with connotations simultaneously Christian and Pagan.[5]

There is another custom, where on the eve of the festival young girls make a Bride (Brighid) doll or Brideog doll of straw, from grains (or reeds) saved from the last year's harvest. They dress the doll in finery and place it in a basket near the fireplace along with a white rod or *slachdan* of birch or willow or a broom—a "magic wand" symbolic of Brighid's ability to control the weather. In the morning if a footstep is seen in the ashes, it is a sign that Brighid herself has been there.

There is also a traditional prohibition on all activities that involve turning wheels.

On Imbolc Eve, the night Brighid comes by to add her blessings and healing powers to these objects, I like to leave a candle outside in the snow (here in New England it's still snowy in February), a bride doll made of wheat (which I later place on the altar or hang from the ceiling), a *brat* (cloak) to wear when ill during the year, and clooties* that can be tied on to a sick person or animal.†

---

*Remember the rag tree described earlier? As noted earlier, Scots call these strips of cloth clooties; in Ireland they are just rags.

†Fun fact—the founder of the Amherst Irish Association here in Massachusetts says she leaves her knickers out on Imbolc Eve so Brighid will empower them. They then become her "power panties"!

Figure 19. A bride doll made of straw and some wild grasses. I make one every year at Imbolc, after soaking the wheat in the tub overnight. Prayers and wishes are breathed into the knots as I tie them.
Photo by Kate Devlin.

One year when the Druids came to my house for the Lughnasad camp, it was a time of drought. I felt terrible for the wild animals and birds; streams had dried up, and the ground was cracked and hard. We decided to do a water ritual, and everyone put food out on a big rock in the forest as an offering. I took down four of the wheat bride dolls I had from former years, which had been hanging over the altar in my bedroom. We put one bride doll into the dry creek bed, one into the fire, one on a stone, and one in a tree. That night it rained for the first time in many weeks. The little creek was filled with water and the tired-looking leaves became plump and green again.

The Ritual of the Dying Ember

Traditional Irish Druid Emer Clougherty told the Tribe of the Oak of a custom that she and her forebears practiced at Imbolc. She said that for her family this was the most important festival of the year. She called her family observance the Ritual of the Dying Ember.

At the end of winter, at the First Quarter Moon, all the women would come to the grandmother's house and leave baskets of food in the scullery. Then they would sit, chat, knit, and wait for the sun to set. The door was left open, and no lights were kindled. The hearth-fire was allowed to gradually die down, and as the room grew darker, the women's stories grew darker too, turning to tales of sadness, anger, and grief.

Eventually songs of mourning were begun by the grandmother with all the women joining in. A small girl was taken by the hand to the well outside where water was drawn, and the girl was told to carry it carefully back to the house. The girl then washed her grandmother's tears with the water. An aunt would hand the girl a candle, and the grandmother used the last hot ember to light it. Then the aunt placed the lit candle on the table and the fireplace was swept completely clean, the only time this happened all year. A new fire was constructed and then lit from the candle, and finally all the other candles in the house were lit from the new fire. Feasting followed.

While this ritual of purification was going on, the men stayed outside in a circle, protecting the women so that the women could safely channel the sorrows of the whole community. The role of the men was to create the space and provide the protection so the women could channel the grief, and this is also why women do the keening at funerals.

Beltaine

Beltaine (May 1 in modern Pagan practice) is the portal between winter and summer and the start of the light half of the year. Just as at Samhain, the opposite festival in the ritual wheel of the year, the walls between the worlds are thin and the Fairies, ancestors and other Spirits easily cross to this side of the veil. We humans can choose to sleep under a flowering Elder or a flowering Apple tree to make contact with the Spirits. Some will do this by choice and others will avoid the practice at all costs, out of fear.

Beltaine marks the time when the weather is warm enough to send the cows back up to the hills and summer pastures. In Celtic areas such as Ireland, the blooming of the Hawthorn tree was once the signal for the advent of warmer weather. In my opinion every Druid should have at least one Hawthorn tree in their garden, to properly calculate the

Figure 20. A flowering Hawthorn on Smeardon Down, on the western edge of Dartmoor.
This image was shared by Nilfanion, CC BY-SA 3.0/ Wikimedia Commons.

timing of the festival in their area. Where I live the Hawthorns don't bloom until at least mid-May.

There are different ways to calculate the date of this Holy Day. Some believe in astronomical calculations, meaning the exact date between the Spring Equinox and the Summer Solstice (though it's hard for me to imagine Iron Age farmers doing that). Others simply follow the calendar, and still others wait for the blooming of the Hawthorn. It's not really Beltaine in my eyes until I see the first white blossoms on the trees.

In ancient times, once the Hawthorns had bloomed the cows were ritually purified and blessed for their journey back up to the summer pastures. In Indo-European thinking cows are lunar animals, that is, animals that contain a sacred liquid: *soma*, or milk. Lunar, watery cows were passed between two large bonfires that had to be close enough together that a white cow would have her fur singed brown. In this way the two basic building blocks of creation came together, fire and water, and the greatest potential for magic and transformation was put into motion.

The procession to the summer grazing started at dawn when everyone gathered their belongings and flocks. The sheep went first, then the cattle, and then the goats and horses. Songs of protection were sung over the herds as a type of incantation.

Here is an excerpt from a Scottish song from *Carmina Gadelica* called "An Saodachadh" (the driving):

> *The protection of Odhran the dun be yours,*
> *The protection of Brigit the Nurse be yours,*
> *The protection of Mary the Virgin be yours,*
> *In marshes and in rocky ground,*
> *In marshes and in rocky ground.*
>
> *The keeping of Ciaran the swart be yours,*
> *The keeping of Brianan the yellow be yours,*
> *The keeping of Diarmaid the brown be yours,*
> *A-sauntering the meadows,*
> *A-sauntering the meadows.*
>
> *The safeguard of Fionn mac Cumhall be yours,*
> *The safeguard of Cormac the shapely be yours,*
> *The safeguard of Conn and Cumhall be yours*
> *From wolf and from bird-flock*
> *From wolf and bird-flock . . .*[6]

The capturing of sunlight in water is an important part of this festival. Women gather May dew at dawn and wash their faces in it to become beautiful. Dew gathered on Beltaine morning after it has received the Sun's rays is kept all year as a healing agent and the first person to the well on Beltaine morning scoops up the water as the sunlight hits it, capturing the "sun in the water" as a blessing.

May Butter, made from milk gathered on Beltaine morn, is thought to have special healing powers (ideally the butter is made before dawn in order to avoid the attention of the Fairies and Witches who might want to steal it).

In British and Germanic areas the May Pole is erected, a phallic symbol composed of a tall tree nestled firmly inside a deep feminine hole. The May Pole is often decorated with blooming Hawthorn at the top, but on no account should blooming "thorn be brought into the home because if one does that the Fairies might come in with it!"

In Ireland it is the May Bush (Hawthorn) with its dyed, sun-yellow eggshells, along with ribbons and yellow flowers such as Marsh Marigold that honors the Sun. It is placed in a communal area and danced around, with a bonfire nearby. Primroses are scattered in front of doors to confuse the Fairies who are known to be extra active at this time because they love the blooms so much that they will become enchanted by their presence and lose interest in coming inside the house.

In British areas Morris Men (and women) dance in the dawn on Beltaine morn, tapping the ground with sticks to wake up any still-slumbering Earth energies while Holy Wells are dressed with ferns and flowers.

When I celebrated the Beltaine fire festival in my grove we would set up two fire altars, one dedicated to the Solar God Belenos and another dedicated to the Solar Goddess Belissama. We danced around the fires in a figure eight procession and, when the flames died down a bit, leapt the fires or stepped over the coals for luck.

A note of caution: it is very bad luck to be handfasted or married at Beltaine. Frivolity, sexual dalliance, and a mischievous atmosphere do not make a sound basis for a strong union. Successful marriages are supposed to be contracted at Lughnasad (see below).

Lughnasad

Lughnasad, from the Old Irish, is a combination of *Lug* (the God Lugh) and *násad* (an assembly). It is the celebration of the beginning of the harvest that can take place any time from the end of July to the second week of August. Some like to celebrate July 31–August 1; others will calculate the exact astronomical date between Summer Solstice and the Fall Equinox.

By tradition the feast of Lughnasad was instituted by the God Lugh (see page 55 for more on Lugh) in honor of his foster mother Tailtiu, who died as a result of her labors in clearing a great plain so that the tribes could plant their seeds and grow food. It's not hard to think of this as a Celtic reimagining of a possibly older story about the Land Goddess who sacrifices her energy and her body so that the people may eat.

At this time it is respectful to stop and pay homage to the Spirits and natural forces that have labored all summer to grow the flowers, fruits, and vegetables, and especially the wheat, so that we and all nature can have life. Here is a summary of some of the activities that were once done to honor the first fruits of the harvest from Máire MacNeill's *The Festival of Lughnasa*:

> Solemn cutting of the first of the corn of which an offering would be made to the deity by bringing it up to a high place and burying it; a meal of the new food and of bilberries* of which everyone must partake; a sacrifice of a sacred bull, a feast of its flesh, with some ceremony involving its hide, and its replacement by a young bull; a ritual dance-play perhaps telling of a struggle for a goddess and a ritual fight; an installation of a head on top of the hill and a triumphing over it by an actor impersonating Lugh; another play representing the confinement by Lugh of the monster blight or famine; a three-day celebration presided over by the brilliant young god or his human representative. Finally, a ceremony indicating that the interregnum was over, and the chief god in his right place again.[7]

Traditionally it was a time of great fairs, games, and competitions when even poets challenged each other, to see who would emerge the champion. Contracts were pledged under the guidance of a Druid, and

---

*Bilberries are a type of blueberry.

handfastings and marriages were solemnized. It made sense to wait for Lughnasad to bind yourself to a marriage partner—by then you would know if he had fertile fields, healthy cows, strong horses, and the strength and wit to bring in a good harvest.

Lughnasad was also a time for horse racing and horse trading. At Beltaine we saw how cows, which are watery, lunar animals, were led between two fires in an act of ritual purification. At Lughnasad it was horses, creatures of fire, that were led through water as an act of sacramental ablution. Once again there was the coming together of fire and water, the basic building blocks of creation, and the greatest potential for magic and transformation.

Lughnasad is a good time to make offerings to live water such as ponds, lakes, and streams, in thanks for their life-giving properties. Rain at Lughnasad is considered a blessing—many crops are still in the ground and the harvest is not yet safely complete.

August 1st was called Lammas Day in English areas (from the Anglo-Saxon *hlaf-mas*, "loaf-mass"), the festival of the wheat harvest and the celebration of first fruits at the start of the harvest season. This was once the time when tenants presented freshly harvested wheat to their landlord and a loaf made from the new crop was brought to church to be blessed. Afterward the sanctified loaf was taken home and broken into four sections that were hidden in the four corners of the barn as a charm to protect the grain.

Bilberries, which become ripe at this time, are important to these celebrations. Bilberries are picked and eaten fresh on Bilberry Sunday (the Sunday closest to Lughnasad) or made into pies and wine.

Holy Wells are circumambulated *deiseal* (sunwise, or clockwise) and offerings placed there. On Garland Sunday important stones in the landscape and near wells are decorated with garlands of flowers and wheat. High hills are climbed and offerings are left at the top in honor of many-skilled Lugh, or of the Sun that nurtures the harvest (please note, the idea that Lugh is a Sun God is inaccurate and dates from Victorian times).

A Traditional Irish Method to Time Your Druid Festivals

We have seen how different Druid groups calculate varying dates for the Holy Days. To add to this, Emer Clougherty, a traditional Irish Druid, shared yet one more method to fix the date. According to her the Moon phase was the most important determinant of the day for ancient Druids. In her system the Samhain festival (where our calendar starts) falls at the end of the last lunar month of the year (at the dark of the Moon). This makes sense as Samhain was a fearful time when most people would have tried hard to stay at home to avoid the wandering ghoulies and ghosties.

> Imbolc occurs at the first quarter of the fourth lunar month, fitting for a fire festival of new beginnings and the start of spring.
>
> Beltaine falls on the full Moon of the seventh lunar month, perfect for a big party when friends and relations will be travelling far and staying up all night. You don't want them stumbling around in the dark, do you?
>
> Lughnasad is the last quarter of the tenth lunar month, a fitting place to put a festival that marks the beginning of fall and the gradual onset of darker days.

Working with thirteen lunar months means that some years will have twelve Months (I call them Moonths) and some will have thirteen. If things start drifting, the Midwinter Solstice is always somewhere in the second lunar Month.

For me it is easy to imagine that ancient cow farmers would have been very aware of which phase the Moon was in, day to day. They probably used the Moon phases as their calendar. I just can't imagine them making complicated astronomical calculations to determine the precise midpoints between the equinoxes and solstices.

The Solstices and Equinoxes

The solstices and equinoxes do have folkloric and spiritual customs attached to them, but they are not considered to be high holy days for most Celtic Druids. These are astronomical, sky-oriented events, rather than a celebration of the agricultural cycle. However, modern Druids do flock to ancient Neolithic temples such as Stonehenge, which has both a Winter Solstice sunset and a Summer Solstice sunrise orientation. Newgrange in Meath, Ireland, is another popular ancient site with its unique "light box" that lets in the Winter Solstice Sun. But these are not "Celtic" monuments, they belong to a different time and religion. So, what evidence do we have for Celtic practices at these astronomical turning points?

The Gallo-Roman Coligny Calendar has the date of Winter Solstice marked. It is called Deuoriuos Riuri (Great Divine Feast of Frost) so there must have been some kind of observance at that time.

In Wales there is still the tradition of the Mari Lwyd (the Grey Mare), a female horse's skull fixed to a pole and decorated with ribbons and bells that is carried from house to house at the time of Winter Solstice. The person carrying the skull is covered with a blanket to disguise their human appearance, and the jaws of the Mari clack open and shut as the figure walks about, accompanied by other guisers, her Otherworldly retinue and helpers.

Figure 21. A photo of a Mari Lwyd, from the Welsh tradition.
Image shared by R. Fiend, CC BY-SA 3.0/Wikimedia Commons.

At each house they come to, the guisers ask to be let in. After a back-and-forth riposte, the Mari and her company are finally admitted. Then the Mari begins to lunge and snap at the inhabitants, especially at the younger women. Only when a small child offers the figure a sweet does the mayhem finally stop. Could this be a ritualized visit from the Land Goddess herself, bringing luck and fertility to each home and especially to the women?

Another folk ritual is the Hunting of the Wren. These days no wrens are killed, but centuries ago a wren would have been hunted down and stoned to death. The little corpse was then laid in a decorated box and carried from house to house, accompanied by a retinue of musicians, dancers, and singers, including a White Mare figure.

When admitted to the home, the Wren Boys danced and sang, and asked for money or drinks. At the end of their peregrinations through town, they buried the wren either on the land of the stingiest person in the village, which was considered very bad luck, or in a neutral, liminal area such as the black shore of the sea (between the line of seaweed and the water).

It is worth noting that the wren is known as the Druid Bird. Though tiny, a wren once took part in a contest to see who would be named King of the Birds. The eagle flew highest of all, but when it could climb no farther, a tiny wren that had nestled in the eagle's feathers popped out and flew higher still, using its brains rather than brawn to win the title.

The killing of the wren may be a folk reference to killing off the old Pagan ways and the magic of the Druids. Or it could be related to the Indo-European idea of the foundational sacrifice that created the world, and which must be repeated to keep the world going through the deadly cold of winter.

Spring Equinox

In Welsh tradition golden, round cross buns are shared on Good Friday. These are a pretty obvious reference to the golden orb of the Sun, with an equal-armed solar cross piped on as added decoration. In Brittany there is a ritual where old pots are hung from strings and a blindfolded man tries to smash them to pieces with a stick, which may be a way of dispelling the last shards of winter. In Orkney they say that the Sea God Teran and the Sea Goddess Mither o' the Sea do battle at this time. The evidence of their struggle is seen in the gales and storms of spring. Sea Mither eventually wins, ushering in the season of gentle summer and warm seas.

In spring, hens and wild birds begin laying eggs again, which is why we celebrate Easter with colored eggs. Rabbits reproduce like, well, rabbits, revealing the basis for the Easter Bunny. Easter Eggs and Easter Bunnies are a Germanic spring custom but ubiquitous in all once-Celtic areas today.

Eggs are a powerful magical tool—capable of transforming from a liquid-containing orb into a flesh and blood chicken. When a fertile egg is removed from the nest and planted in the grain store instead of being allowed to mature into a fowl, it lends its transformative power and magic to the grain. Images can be painted on eggs and the eggs buried in the ground at this time to manifest dreams and wishes.

Summer Solstice

By custom medicinal herbs are gathered on the longest day of the year because at that time they have special powers. This makes sense because at the height of summer the potency of the herb will be drawn upward toward the Sun and the aerial parts of the plant. Roots are gathered in the fall when the plant's energy has moved back down toward the soil.

Herb magic would once have been a Druidical function, and we can still collect the plants in the old traditional way: taken with the left hand while wearing loose clothing and using no metal. A nonmetallic cutting tool such as a bone or crystal blade will be the least offensive to the Spirits, and the plants must be transferred to the right hand and then placed onto a cloth—and never be allowed to touch the ground. A thanks offering of milk, cider, or honey should be given to the Earth to compensate her for her loss.

In Brittany medicinal plants are classified as if coming from the body of the slain God (see the story of Airmid on page 47).

> Psychotropic herbs form the head of the God, for example Henbane (*Hyoscyamus niger*), Nightshades (*Solanum* spp.*)*, and spiritually important Druidic herbs like Vervain (*Verbena officinalis, V. hastata, V. urticifolia*).
>
> The blood of the God is found in vulneries and anticoagulants such as Saint John's wort (*Hypericum perforatum*) and Yarrow (*Achillea millefolium*). Saint John's wort even "bleeds" red when the flowers are crushed in your hand or are made into oil.
>
> The inner organs of the God are symbolized by herbs that help the digestion, the reproductive organs and the organs of elimination, such as Male Fern (*Dryopteris filix-mas*) which is anti-parasitic, and the limbs by Mugwort (*Artemisia vulgaris*) for inflammation, and wounds.[8]

At Summer Solstice bonfires were once ubiquitous; on hilltops, at crossroads, near Holy Wells, and on tribal borders. The fires were lit at sunset. Other activities with sacred fire included throwing lit torches into the air, rolling fire wheels down hills, carrying torches around the boundaries of the land and in between the rows of crops, and spreading embers and ashes from a sacred fire among the crops—a type of ritual purification by fire. Torches were affixed to walls and to the house and barn, and left burning all night.[9]

In Ireland the longest day is sacred to the Goddess Áine (see page 38) and her sister Grian (Sun) (see page 49) possibly the Summer and Winter Suns, who are said to have a sanctuary on the mountain called Cnoc Áine. On Saint John's Eve folk would gather there to observe the Moon and then march through the fields and cattle herds with lit torches.[10]

Mallow (*Malva* spp.) leaves are picked on Midsummer Eve and friends and relatives are touched with them. The leaves are later offered to the sacred fire. It is worth noting that Mallows are demulcent (soothing to tissue) and are magically known to pull in good Spirits.

Protective Birch branches are hung over the household door and over the barn entrance. Saint John's Wort is worn, hung in the home, smoked over the ritual fire, and kept as a protective talisman all year.

Fall Equinox

Fall Equinox is the middle of the harvest in southern Celtic areas, though in Scotland the 29th of September became the Feast of Saint Michael, who is a Christianization of Lugh (see Lugh on page 55). All over the Celtic lands, the high places once sacred to Lugh became "Michael Mounts" or churches were deliberately placed on top of them. Because Scotland is farther north, this time period more closely resembles Lughnasad and the beginning of the harvest in more southern climes.

At Michaelmas, as at Lughnasad in southern areas, horses and horse racing were popular in Scotland. Even the stealing of a horse for the competition was tolerated, so long as it was returned by the next morning. Women dug carrots and shared bunches of them with their lovers, an obvious phallic reference. The carrots were also treats for the horses.

When the last sheaf of the harvest was ritually taken, blindfolded harvesters stood with their backs to it and threw their sickles at it until its "neck" was cut. The power of the Land Spirits was retained in that last ceremonial sheaf, which was further consecrated by being woven into a corn dolly fashioned to resemble a hare, a mare, or a human Goddess figure.

The sheaf was kept for a year and then burned once a new corn dolly was made, if the harvest was good. In that case the new dolly was called the Corn Maiden, and she was a guest of honor at the harvest feast. But if the harvest was bad the dolly was called the Cailleach (hag, old woman) and buried secretly.

Once again, the Orkney Sea God Teran and the Sea Goddess Mither o' the Sea do battle. This time Teran wins out and harsh winter gales and cold seas set in.

Magical Techniques
of the Druids

Draíocht (DREE-ocht), the Druidic art, Druidism, magic, is a little-understood aspect of the Druid path. In ancient times when Druids were a highly respected caste within Celtic society, draíocht was a highly specialized and learned skill. As the Christian religion and morality took hold, the sacred status of the Druid fell to that of mere magician. By the year 448 CE, at the fourteenth synod at Armagh, anyone performing soothsaying or fortune-telling was required to do penance. Druid magic was included, and the Druid's status in the laws fell.

Before the Christian debasement, an important magical function of the Druids had been to ensure the health and prosperity of the land. This was achieved by carefully crafted sacrifices. Regular sacrifice was needed to give energy back to the Goddesses and Gods, the Elementals, and to all the forces that create the cosmos. It was a gift from the human realm to the forces that create the living land. As those forces worked to feed the people, the people gave back in a reciprocal relationship managed by the Druids.

The universe itself was understood to have been born from a primal sacrifice—that of a giant who was dismembered and whose body parts became all of creation. But that foundation sacrifice gradually lost energy and became run down, so other sacrifices had to be re-enacted.

When an animal was offered up, each part of it gave its energies to a different cosmic realm. For example, the brain became the clouds, the face became the Sun, the hair became the vegetation, and so on. This reciprocal offering of "energy" was a common facet of many Indo-European cultures. It did not necessarily mean sacrificing an animal, though that was possible. Other sacrifices could be done, such as giving the first fruits of the harvest back to the land at Lughnasad or making a corn dolly from the last sheaf of the harvest, ritually cutting it, and burying it back in the ground the next spring.

Modern Druids, I hasten to add, do not kill anything (other than possibly pulling vegetables or cutting grain). But we do continue to make sacrifices by placing food offerings or art works into the fire or placing fruits, flowers, and silver into the waters. We also sacrifice our time and energy to teach and promote the Druid path and to do charitable work for our communities.

Some Specific Druidic Magical Techniques

Crane Magic

Corrguinecht was a type of magic where a Druid would stand in the shape or posture of a crane, on one leg with one arm extended and one eye closed. The heron's, or crane's, stance was enacted to send out a potent satire or curse.

The Druidic Cloak of Invisibility

Druids had a mantle of concealment or cloak of invisibility that they used to make someone invisible. Druids could also raise a Druid Mist (Ceo Druidechta, Modern Irish: Ceo Draíochta), a type of fog that hid persons and objects. Every Sidhe mound was said to have a protective fog of enchantment around it, to protect it from mortal eyes.

Seeing

A Frithir (Scottish for "Seer") was a person who could "See" the place and condition of lost animals and people. A *frith* was done on the first Monday of the quarter, just before sunrise—for example, the Monday after each fire festival. The Frithir would go barefoot, fasting, and with a bare head and closed eyes, to the doorstep. He or she would stand there with one hand on each doorjamb, invoke the Goddesses and Gods, and then open their eyes, looking straight ahead. Whatever the Seer saw before them became the omen, or "seeing."

If the Seer saw a man standing that meant good health, a man lying down denoted illness. A woman standing signified bad luck approaching, but a woman passing by or approaching the door was good luck. A woman with red hair meant trouble, while a woman with black hair meant good fortune. Blondes, especially those with blue eyes, were a problem because they were very attractive to the Fairies and could draw them to the house. To see a woman with brown hair was the best luck of all.

Any person or animal getting up meant improving health, lying down meant sickness or death. A bird flying by, especially if it was a lark or a dove, was a good omen. A cock coming toward the Seer implied good luck, a duck safety for sailors, a raven death. It was bad luck to have a crow look down the chimney, for that meant that someone within the house was soon to die. To see a pig or a boar was good luck, and to see the totem animal of one's clan always meant good fortune. Regarding seeing horses, this rhyme survives: "A white horse for land, a gray horse for sea, a bay horse for burial, a brown horse for sorrow." And if a cat walked away from the fire, that meant a storm was coming, but if the cat washed its face, that meant rain was on its way.

A Seer could also stare at a fire or gaze through the blade bone of a sheep's shoulder to read an omen. She might hear the cry of a dying person, meaning a death was coming, or smell a meal that wouldn't be cooked for months, predicting a future gathering.

If a true Seer was having a vision and they touched another person, that person would also see the same vision. But to have "second sight" was considered a curse because if you had it, you could never see people just as they were in the moment—rather you would see their future and their death.

More Magical Skills of a Seer

By the eighth year of Bardic training in Ireland, a Seer was expected to have mastered these three skills: *imbas forosnai* (IM-vas forOSH-naee), "illumination between the palms" or "palm knowledge of enlightenment"; *díchetal do chennaib* (DIH-hedahl tho CHEN-naee), "recital from the ends of the fingers," "declaration from the ends of the bones," or "poem from the ends of the fingers"; and *teinm laida* (TAIN-v LOItha) "illumination of song." Details of these poetic techniques can be found in the late-medieval *Yellow Book of Lecan* (*Leabhar Buidhe Leacáin*).

Imbas forosnai is a composite of the words *imbas*, meaning "poetic inspiration that descends," and *forosnai*, meaning "illuminated" (i.e., the fire in the head). It is a technique where sacred poetry that imparts spiritual wisdom is composed spontaneously.

Díchetal do chennaib is a spontaneous uttering of poetic prophecy using the tips of the fingers as a mnemonic device: composing and reciting at the same time. This particular poetic skill was never outlawed by the church because it did not involve contact with Spirits.

Teinm laida is an altered state brought on by repetitive chanting or singing where the mind and body become synchronized to an external rhythm, and the person transcends normal perception (think of the repetitive singing of a mantra during an Indian Kirtan, where hours of chanting produce an altered state of heightened focus and inner peace).

These techniques are very different from memorized poetry or poetry written using intellectual skills. They are a type of inspired poetry that descends quickly, as a gift from the Goddesses and Gods.

Poetic Magic

Incubating a Poem in the Dark

We know of a technique where the poet went into a dark room or under a leather hide, pronounced an invocation or prayer over their hands, and then placed their hands crosswise over their face and eyes. Then they went into a trance or a meditative state. Without warning the covering hide was suddenly removed by a second person, which triggered spontaneous visions or poetic speech and prophecy. Secret knowledge was sometimes revealed by this method.

Yet another poetic exercise involved the poet chewing on a piece of raw flesh from a dog, cat, pig, or bull and then placing the chewed meat on a flagstone behind the door as an offering to the Spirits (the church REALLY didn't like this one!). By eating raw flesh the poet was no longer fully human and had greater contact with the vast, numinous Spirit of Nature. Answers to questions were achieved with this technique.

In the *tarb feis* (*tarb fesh* or bull feast) a bull was sacrificed, and everyone feasted on the meat while the Seer was sewn into the hide (flesh side out) and left there for three days. He or she was expected to emerge with a prophecy, an inspired poem, or the answer to an important question like who the next ruler should be.

In Scotland there was a ritual called *taghairm* (spiritual echo or calling up the dead) (tah-gerim) where the Seer was wrapped in the hide of a newly slain cow or ox and laid before a waterfall. A question was asked of the Seer, who lay for hours with the Cloak of Knowledge around them. The sound of the waterfall and the heat of the cow hide brought on a trance where the Spirits could speak directly to the Seer. This ritual was in use until the seventeenth century.

Taghairm na daoine (tah-gerim nah DAH-oheen) (spirit call) involved the Seer being placed inside a large cauldron outside of a burial ground. The Seer would call the dead to appear and kept it up until a ghost made itself manifest so that the seer could communicate with them.

Notice that all these techniques resemble a journey back to the womb—the poet being placed in darkness under a skin covering, sitting in a large cauldron, or sewn up into a leather bag. This appears to be another version of what I call Salmon Wisdom, discussed later, where the poet goes back to Source to retrieve an answer.

All Poetry Is Magic and All Magic Is Poetry

For the ancients, poetry and magic were the same thing because once you defined something poetically, you had called it into being. Born from the fire of imbas, the creative fire became manifested reality. A skilled poet did not need to rely on techniques or methods—they could go into trance anywhere and without a ritual or preparation. For example, on the battlefield.

The *rosc* is a type of spoken poetic spell, a rhetorical chant that did not rhyme but used alliteration instead. *Roscanna* (plural) were employed in battle magic and used to bless, curse, advise, create illusions, discern truth, or interpret dreams. They were also devised to cause sleep or healing. These poems might be recited while in the crane stance (see page 88), were spoken in the present tense, and the speaker said what they wanted, *as if it was already true.*

In other words, the speaker was not asking for something to happen; they were saying that it *already was.*

An Ollamh (OH-lav) was Chief Poet of a tribe and had to protect the ruler from sorcery as well as divine the future. And trained poets were also the masters of satire. They might make fun of someone's appearance, broadcast a blemish, or coin a derogatory nickname. But composing or repeating a satire, making mocking gestures, taunting someone, falsely accusing a person of theft, or spreading a destructive lie about someone dead or alive required a fine of the victim's honor price. The harm could be nullified, however, by broadcasting a praise poem.

If a satire made about a ruler was justified, the ruler had to pay a fine. If it was unjustified, the noble or ruler had to exact compensation or lose face. Remember the seriousness of this; any king who was "blemished" could be fired.

The Glám Dicenn

The *glám dicenn* (GLAHM dickeen), "metrical malediction," "extempore satire," or "blistering satire," is a type of poetic black magic where the poet composes a satire in the shade of a Hawthorn tree without thorns and having a dense, heavy top.

The satire is repeated three times nine times "in the circuit of the Moon" (i.e., twenty-seven times a day, for one month). While chanting the poet would pierce a clay likeness of their target with the thorns from a Hawthorn tree (presumably the now-thornless tree they were standing under).

In another version seven grades of poets would climb to a hilltop before sunrise, and with their backs to a Hawthorn tree and the wind from the north (the direction of battle), they would hold a thorn from the tree in each hand as they chanted a satire.

Divination by Bird Augury

Druids did many different forms of divination such as studying the wind direction, casting Ogham sticks, scrying into water or flames, and cloud divination. Another potent form of divination was ornithomancy, or bird augury. The table on pages 94–95 provides some examples of the divinatory meanings of birds. The call of the wren is particularly significant for Druids, as it is our own bird totem.

Divinatory Meanings of the Call of the Wren

If a wren calls from the east, poets or pious visitors are coming or bringing a message. But if it's pious visitors, they will be discourteous.

If a wren calls from the southeast, jesters are coming.

If from the southwest, ex-freemen are coming.

If from the north, someone dear to you is on the way.

If from the northwest, pious folk are coming.

If from the south, and provided the wren is not between you and the Sun, the slaying of someone dear to you, or unfaithfulness.

If a wren calls at your left ear, it means sex with a young person.

DIVINATORY MEANINGS OF BIRDS

	Bird	Meaning
	Blackbird	A blackbird singing from a high place meant good weather, if from low down, rain.
	Cock	A cock crowing in the afternoon meant a visitor was coming. A cock crowing three times at night meant death or misfortune.
	Crane	Crane was a messenger of the Goddesses and Gods heralding war or death.
	Crow	Crow meant a message from the Otherworld, an omen of change, or death. Faeries will take the form of crows.
	Cuckoo	When the cuckoo sang, spring had arrived.
	Dove	Dove brought love, peace, innocence, faithfulness, and purity.
	Eagle	Eagle represented the High Goddesses and Gods, victory, pride, royalty, authority, and strength.

	Bird	Meaning
	Falcon	Falcon meant aspiration, freedom, and victory.
	Goose	If geese were flying out to sea, good weather was nigh. If geese were cackling loudly, it meant rain. Geese also embody love and domestic skills, as well as protection of the home.
	Hawk	Hawk meant the High Goddesses and Gods, power, royalty, and nobility.
	Hen	A crowing hen meant magic at work, or a powerful woman.
	Swan	To see a swan was lucky. As with all white animals, it meant a visit from the Otherworld.
	Wren	The wren was the king of all birds and the Druid Bird. Its feathers protected against sorcery. The call of the wren is particularly significant for Druids, as it is our own bird totem.

All images in this table are in the public domain.

Divinatory Meanings of the Call of the Wren (cont.)

If a wren calls from behind you, someone is pursuing your spouse.

If from the ground behind you, your spouse will be taken by force.

If from the south behind you, heads of good clergy are coming, or death for noble clergy.

If from the southwest, robbers, evil peasants, or bad women are approaching.

If from the west, wicked relations are on the way.

If from the northwest, a noble hero, a good woman, or a generous person is coming.

If from the north, bad people or wicked youths are nigh.

If from the south, it means sickness and wolves.

If a wren calls from the ground, from a stone, or from a cross, this means the death of a great man.

If wrens call from many crosses, this means a slaughter of men and the number of times they land on the ground will give the number of men. The quarter to which the birds face tells the direction that the dead are from.

Druidic Wisdom Tales
and Poetry

Three foundations of wisdom: discretion in learning, memory in retaining, and eloquence in telling.

ANCIENT IRISH TRIAD

As a Druid you should familiarize yourself with the ancient poems and tales. These will enrich your ritual practice and give you a deep appreciation for the sages who created our tradition. There are many cultures to choose from: the Welsh poetry of Taliesin and the Mabinogion, the traditional corpus of Irish tales, and even Vedic texts like the *Rig Veda* and the *Bhagavad-Gita*. Below is a small sampling of the kinds of writings that are available to us from the ancient lore.

To begin this chapter I offer a stanza from the *Immacallam in dá Thuarad* (The Colloquy of the Two Sages), which is a twelfth-century example of a bardic competition where two poets are competing for the title of Chief Poet. I think it lays out beautifully the course of study that a true Druid should pursue:

> *And you, O knowledgeable lad, whose son are you?*
> *Nede answered*
> *Not hard: I am the son of poetry,*
> *Poetry son of scrutiny,*
> *Scrutiny son of meditation,*

Meditation son of lore,
Lore son of inquiry,
Inquiry son of investigation,
Investigation son of great knowledge,
Great knowledge son of great sense,
Great sense son of understanding,
Understanding son of wisdom.
Wisdom son of the triple gods of poetry.[1]

Here are samples of two roscanna (short, unrhymed Old Irish verses that use alliteration and meter) as translated by Seán Ó Tuathail. In the first rosc, a section from "Lugh's Crane Magic," Lugh stands on one leg with one eye closed, and one hand behind his back in the corrguinecht (crane stance) and chants a battle spell:

. . . O Fairy-hosts, land of men on guard,
birds of prey rain down (on them), men without
  choice.
Be hindered (the) foreigners. Another (the other)
  company fears,
another company listens, they are very terribly in
  torment,
dark (sad) men (are they). Roaring brightly
  ninefold are we!
Hurrah and Woe! Leftward! O you my beautiful
  ones!
Sacred will be the sustenance after cloud and
  flowers
through its powerful skills of wizards
My battle will not dwindle until (its) end . . .[2]

And here is a portion from "Morigu's (Morrígan's) Prophecy," from after the battle of Moy Tuireadh (Moytura):

Peace to (as high as) the sky
sky to the earth
earth beneath sky
strength in everyone
a cup very full
a fullness of honey
honour enough
summer in winter
spear supported by shield
shields supported by forts
forts fierce eager for battle . . .[3]

The *Audacht Morainn* (Testament of Morann) ascribed to Morann mac Móin and addressed to his foster-son Nére to be delivered by him to King Feradach Findfechtnach (King of Ireland from 15 to 36 CE) was written down in the seventh century and before that was in the oral tradition. It is a king-making ceremony where the Druid is giving the new ruler advice on how to be a good king. It's worth studying the whole text in detail—these are just a few of my favorite passages from the manuscript.

In this translation by Fergus Kelly, we here see the Druid telling the king that everything depends upon his truth and justice because without it even the land will suffer:

Let him preserve Truth, it shall preserve him
Let him raise truth, it will raise him.
Let him exalt mercy, it will exalt him.
Let him care for his tribes, they will care for him.
Let him help his tribes, they will help him.
Let him soothe his tribes, they will soothe him.
Tell him, it is through the truth of the ruler that
 plagues [and] great lightnings are kept from
 the people . . .
It is through the truth of the ruler that every heir

plants his house-post in his fair inheritance.
It is through the truth of the ruler that abundances
   of great tree-fruit of the great wood are tasted.
It is through the truth of the ruler that milk-yields
   of great cattle are maintained.
It is through the truth of the ruler that there is
   abundance of every high, tall corn.
It is through the truth of the ruler that abundance
   of fish swim in streams.
It is through the truth of the ruler that fair
   children are well begotten.

And in one of the most helpful passages in the old Irish literature, the Druid bestows this advice about how to rule successfully:

Darkness yields to light
Sorrow yields to joy
An oaf yields to a sage
A fool yields to a wise man
A serf yields to a free man
Inhospitality yields to hospitality
Niggardliness yields to generosity
Meanness yields to liberality
Impetuosity yields to composure
Turbulence yields to submission
A usurper yields to a true lord
Conflict yields to peace
Falsehood yields to justice.[4]

Here is one of my favorite passages from ancient Irish literature, on how to behave among the wise and the foolish, part of a much longer treatise, *Tecosca Cormaic* (The Instructions of King Cormac Mac Airt), which is well worth studying:

Be not too wise, be not too foolish,
be not too conceited, be not too diffident,
be not too haughty, be not too humble,
be not too talkative, be not too silent,
be not too harsh, be not too feeble.
If you be too wise, one will expect (too much) of you;
if you be too foolish, you will be deceived;
if you be too conceited, you will be thought vexatious;
if you be too humble, you will be without honour;
if you be too talkative, you will not be heeded;
if you be too silent, you will not be regarded;
if you be too harsh, you will be broken;
if you be too feeble, you will be crushed.[5]

The *Ashtavakra Gita*

As discussed earlier, we know that the ancient Celtic religion had the same proto-Vedic roots as Hinduism. Druidism and Hinduism have many parallels: fire altars and sacred wells, sacred trees, sacred cows and horses, triple deities, and the same class structure. It is worth noting again that in both cultures the classes were fluid originally. One could climb up or fall down the social ladder depending upon one's learning and behavior.

The Druids of Ord na Darach Gile, the Order of the White Oak,* began studying this text in June of 2009. It represents the best of Indo-European philosophy and is likely close to what the Druids may have actually taught in their groves. *Gita* means "song", implying that this chant was sung by a Bard or sacred singer.

The *Ashtavakra Gita*, or the *Ashtavakra Samhita* as it is sometimes called, is a very ancient Sanskrit text. The translation here by John Richards is just a small section of a much longer work. I urge every Druid to study the full text.

---

*As noted earlier, the Order of the White Oak disbanded in 2014 and Tribe of the Oak took up the mantle and now continues basically the same lesson plans.

Ashtavakra said:

If you are seeking liberation, my son, avoid the objects of the senses like poison and cultivate tolerance, sincerity, compassion, contentment, and truthfulness as the antidote. (1.2)

You do not consist of any of the elements—earth, water, fire, air, or even ether. To be liberated, know yourself as consisting of consciousness, the witness of these. (1.3)

If only you will remain resting in consciousness, seeing yourself as distinct from the body, then even now you will become happy, peaceful and free from bonds. (1.4)

You do not belong to the brahmin or any other caste, you are not at any stage, nor are you anything that the eye can see. You are unattached and formless, the witness of everything—so be happy. (1.5)

Righteousness and unrighteousness, pleasure and pain are purely of the mind and are no concern of yours. You are neither the doer nor the reaper of the consequences, so you are always free. (1.6)

You are the one witness of everything and are always completely free. The cause of your bondage is that you see the witness as something other than this. (1.7)

Since you have been bitten by the black snake, the opinion about yourself that "I am the doer," drink the antidote of faith in the fact that "I am not the doer," and be happy. (1.8)

Burn down the forest of ignorance with the fire of the understanding that "I am the one pure awareness," and be happy and free from distress. (1.9)

That in which all this appears is imagined like the snake in a rope; that joy, supreme joy, and awareness is what you are, so be happy. (1.10)

If one thinks of oneself as free, one is free, and if one thinks of oneself as bound, one is bound. Here this saying is true, "Thinking makes it so." (1.11)[6]

An Introduction to the
Brehon Laws

Three things required of a judge: wisdom, sharpness, knowledge.

THE TRIADS OF IRELAND

The old tribal laws were very precise in terms of what behavior was expected from community members. It is clear that the tribes had a coherent set of rules and ethics long before the Christian missionaries showed up. The Brehon Laws are believed to have originated in the proto-Indo-European *Laws of Manu* (the Vedic *Manava Dharma Shastra*), which is another ancient text that White Oak Druids read and studied, verse by verse, in about 2009.

A great introduction to the subject of Brehon Law is Fergus Kelly's *A Guide to Early Irish Law* (Dublin Institute for Advanced Studies, 1991), which every Druid should read at least once to appreciate how different Celtic Paganism was from what most modern Pagans currently imagine. There was simply no "Do what thou wilt"—because any society where people were running around following their own whims and desires was surely doomed to chaos and failure. The modern Libertarian philosophy of "do your own thing" might work for a weekend Pagan festival, but it spells disaster for a settled farming community.

We have already seen how dependent the ruler was on the Druid by their side. As the ancient lore states, the ruler and Druid were the "two kidneys" of the kingdom; the ruler depended on the Druid to know the correct laws and precedents and the Druid depended on the ruler to be a competent warrior. The justice and truth of the king determined the fate of the land, the people, the weather, and the animals. The king needed the legally trained Druid to advise them on laws and precedents because if the king failed to uphold justice, it was a cosmic catastrophe.

The Brehon Laws were oral before the seventh century and were still in use until the seventeenth century in Ireland. Thousands of years before the Magna Carta was even dreamed of, the old tribal laws had rules for the behavior of kings who could be deposed if they became blemished in body or by bad behavior.

Because Ireland was never conquered by Rome, and despite the suppression by the English, the Brehon Laws still give us a fairly good idea of what ancient tribal values were for almost three thousand years. They closely resemble the Germanic tribal laws in the way fines were paid in livestock (and some scholars say that most Germans were actually Celts, and one theory holds that Celtic culture may have developed in Austria).

There are similarities to Hinduism again in the Brehon Laws: for example, in the practice of fasting against a person of greater influence to shame them into providing restitution. This mirrors the Hindu ritual of sitting *dharna*, a ritual that continues to this day in India. It includes a fast undertaken at the door of a more powerful offender to obtain justice, respond to a criminal case, or pay a debt. Even a jilted bride left at the altar may fast against her wayward fiancé.

In the Irish laws there were penalties such as blush-fines for wrongly satirizing someone and rules for neighborly conduct and behavior. There were laws pertaining to assemblies and to funeral games and for restitution in the case of theft, injury, or murder. Women are shown to have had a much better social position than Greek and Roman women of the same time. And there were laws pertaining to the protection of trees (see Peter Quandt's chapter beginning on page 211 for more on the tree laws).

Here is a small selection of some of the topics that the laws covered, just to give you an idea:

Land Laws

There was an obligation to weed and clear the roads every three years, in preparation for the assembly.

The worth of land was estimated by the absence of Briars, Blackthorn, and Burdock.

A nearby forest, mill, mine, road, river, mountain, or pool for cattle added value to the price of land.

Land near a chieftain's home or close to a monastery was determined the most valuable.

Laws Pertaining to Women

If the woman had not agreed to an assignation, and she screamed, he was guilty.

Marriage Laws

A groom was required to pay a bride-price of land, cattle, horses, and coins to the father of the bride.

When a woman decided to divorce, she could take with her all the property she had brought to the marriage, anything her husband had given her, and any wealth she had accrued by her own efforts.

There were nine kinds of marriage. Some of these were planned unions and others happened by default, but all were considered binding and legal.

- The union of joint property where both spouses brought equal goods to the marriage and both spouses had equal authority. This was most respectable form of marriage.
- The union of a woman on man where the woman contributed very little property, and he was in charge.
- The union of a man on woman where the man brought very little property, and she was in charge.

- The union of a man visiting where he came to her home with her kin's consent.
- The union where the woman left with the man but without her kin's consent.
- The union where the woman was secretly visited without her kin's consent.
- The union where the woman was abducted.
- Union by rape (this one is especially repugnant to modern sensibilities).
- The union of two persons with intellectual disabilities or mental illness.

If two mentally ill persons chose to marry, both the tribe of the groom and the tribe of the bride were responsible for their upkeep.

In the event a marriage failed, the bride and groom each kept the land, animals, and goods they brought to the union.

A husband who failed his wife in bed through impotence, a preference for boys, or corpulence, had to pay a fine, or she could divorce him.

A husband who denied his pregnant wife food out of neglect was required to pay a fine.

Laws Pertaining to Children

A child's status was the same as that of their parents, and there was no distinction between "legitimate" and "illegitimate" children—even those of concubines received an inheritance.

Children were to be fostered out to learn professions such as medicine, law, poetry, farming, and warrior skills.

Children who had been fostered out had to be returned to their parents when of an age to marry: fourteen for a girl, seventeen for a boy.

Laws Pertaining to Injuries and Physicians

Injuries and restitution were assessed based on the amount of blood shed—from the half shell of a hazelnut to the half shell of a hen's egg.

The doctor's house had to be built over a running stream with four doors that opened out.

No fools, drunks, scolds, grunting pigs, or barking dogs could disturb the doctor's house.

If the doctor failed to heal a wound, he or she was required to return the fee or pay a fine.

Other Miscellaneous Laws

The poet could not overcharge for a poem.

If a hen trespassed into an herb garden, the fine was an oatcake and a side dish of butter or bacon.

Elders had to be provided with one oatcake a day and sour milk, a bath every twentieth night, and seventeen sticks of firewood for the fire.

The laws of hospitality held that "the first drink at an alehouse was free" and every inn had to supply three kinds of meat—plus provide torches along the way so that travelers would not get lost.

The rules of hospitality were also that guests had to be fed, with no questions asked, and it was illegal to offer food in which there was a dead mouse or a weasel.

Every harper had to be given land, elevating them to noble status.

Creditors were required to return jewelry for the duration of the assembly so that a debtor wouldn't suffer humiliation.

Each Brehon was allotted time to speak, long or short, according to his or her dignity and status.

Brehon Laws and Restorative Justice

Three signs of compassion: to understand a child's complaint, to not disturb an animal that is lying down, to be cordial to strangers.

ANCIENT IRISH TRIAD

While it's impossible for modern Druids to live in strict accordance to the Brehon Laws, and indeed many of the laws are products of their time that we *wouldn't* want to go back to, we can still admire the wisdom of the philosophy of restorative justice under which many of the laws were structured. Restorative justice—the idea of bringing together those most affected by a criminal act, such as the offender, the victim, and community members—is a concept that is only starting to be appreciated in modern jurisprudence. The Brehon Laws would be an important and telling study for crafting new laws designed to restore communities.

As we can see from the ancient laws, hospitality was a virtue, persons who were hungry were even allowed to take food from someone's land without penalty. The community had the responsibility to care for children and the elderly and there were fines for harming trees and for killing animals such as dogs.

Druids of today seek to follow the spirit, if not the letter, of these laws by seeing trees and all of nature as sentient and worthy of respect. Druids seek to perceive the sacred in all people and animals.

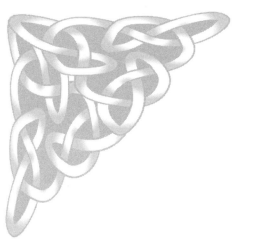
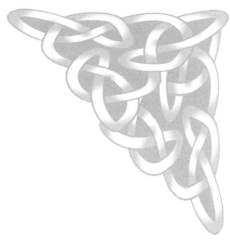

PART 2

Becoming a Druid

How to Practice Druidic Arts, Magic,
and Spritualily

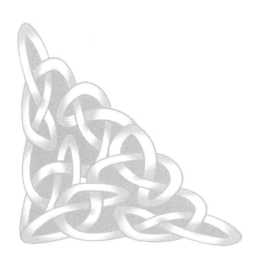

The Tools of a Druid

Three foundations of judgement: bold design, frequent practice, frequent mistakes.

THE TRIADS OF IRELAND

Different types of Druids place varying degrees of value on specific Druidic tools. In "What a Druid Is and Is Not" we got a sense of some of the different schools of thought in modern Druidry and you can look to those as an indicator of which tools might be important to a given type of Druid. For example, if you are a Hedge Druid, that is, a Druid who works with objects and ideas found in their immediate environment, you will likely work with just the materials you find in your nearby landscape. For example, five acorns or pebbles can define a sacred space, and a simple stick might suffice for a wand or staff. A Celtic Reconstructionist Druid will likely research sickles, Iron Age costumes, and other historically based paraphernalia to enhance their ritual practice. If you want to add a bit of artistic flair to your kit, a number of suggestions follow.

The more devotion and personal effort that you put into crafting a magical tool, the more likely you will get good results. Then the tool will *know* you and understand what you are trying to achieve. You want your personal signature to be on everything you use for magic and ritual. That's why it's not advisable to run out and buy all your ritual tools ready-made by someone else. If purchasing robes or a cape, at least add a few stitches here and there, with your own hands. If you buy a drum, paint it with Celtic knotwork symbols or Ogham letters to make it uniquely yours.

The Mystical Tools of a Druid

Your first magical tool is the crane bag. According to Irish tradition, the original *corrbolg*, or crane bag, was made by Manannán MacLir to hold treasures such as his knife and shirt, the king of Scotland's shears, the king of Lochlainn's helmet, the bones of Assal's swine, and the girdle of a great whale's back. At high tide these treasures were visible in the sea, but at ebb tide they vanished.

Modern commentators speculate that the bag may have contained the letters of the Ogham alphabet, the Ogham ciphers having been suggested by the legs of flying cranes. I live in a wet, boggy area of New England, and I have been fortunate to observe cranes as they foraged for their food. Cranes are liminal animals that stick their bill into the mud to fish, patiently stand still for lengths of time in the water, waiting for prey, and they can fly in the air. In other words, they span the Three Worlds.

We have seen earlier the potent form of Celtic magic known as corrguinecht, a form of crane magic, where the practitioner stands on one leg with one eye closed and one arm extended. Some accounts also note the other hand behind the back. In this posture Druids imitate the intense focus of a crane as it seeks its quarry. Placing their body half in this world and half in the Otherworld, beyond use, using this focused almost yogic stance, they send targeted blessings or curses.

A Crane Bag

The crane bag is a small leather bag about the size of your palm. It can be larger but ideally you will wear it attached to a belt or carry it in a pouch, so don't get carried away with making something huge.

Your bag is unique, so once it is made you will personalize it with symbols that are meaningful to you. Triple spirals are very Druidic, as is the three-ray Awen symbol. You can also decorate your bag with Ogham symbols.

Snakes are appropriate as well, the snake being a symbol of transformation and rebirth, because snakes regularly shed their skin and know how to reinvent themselves. *Serpents* is also the ancient name for Druids—as when the missionary Patricius supposedly drove the serpents out of Eire . . . or so it is claimed.

Making a Crane Bag

The number five is a number of completion and wholeness containing the four directions plus the Sacred Center. To begin the construction of your Bag, select earth from five different locations. The first location represents the Sacred Center—a personal power spot, or the place where you were born. Next gather earth from a sacred place in the North, then East, South and West.

Reflect carefully before you gather—these tiny bits of soil should be from places that bring personal power, stability, and assurance to you. Put a teaspoon from each direction, each individually wrapped in a small cloth packet, into your bag.

Next, collect feathers, talons, bones, or any other part of five sacred birds. Please do not harm, kill, or even disturb a bird to achieve this—be creative and find your feathers in nature or beside a bird in captivity. Likewise, collect the fur, teeth, bone, or any other part of five sacred animals. Then collect the bark, leaf, nut, or berry from five sacred trees, and finally the leaf, flower, fruit, or seed from five sacred herbs.

It is entirely up to you which trees, herbs, animals, and birds you choose to place into your crane bag. Whichever you choose, they should be meaningful in a way that enhances your personal power, energy, and spirit. Whenever possible these should be gathered in the wild by your own efforts or be bartered for by labor or trade, rather than purchased.

Once your crane bag is finished it becomes an object of personal power. Do not discuss it, its method of construction, or its contents once it is complete. It may be unobtrusively worn as part of your ritual regalia.

You may elect to place within the bag any other sacred talisman of power that your imbas (poetic knowledge) deems appropriate. Examples would be small statues of deities, herbs such as Dragon's Blood to enliven the mixture, Mistletoe to enhance its magical strength, or the charcoal from an Oak tree that was struck by lightning and survived, to increase its power.

The Serpent Staff

Now you are ready to carve or find in the landscape of nature a wooden serpent staff, also known as a snake stick or Druid wand, which should resemble a snake in its outward appearance. You can awaken it by adding eyes once it has been consecrated after the manner your own imbas suggests—that is, it (and any other of your ritual tools) can be consecrated by passing it through sacred smoke or washing it with a brew of sacred herbs. You might also choose to adorn it with stones or gems to mark important life passages.

The serpent staff should be kept hidden in a pouch or be wrapped in cloth until the time of its use. It is a tool for the sending of *draiocht* (Druid magic) and not to be used lightly or in the sight of persons who would disrespect or confuse its meaning.

A consecrated serpent staff can be further empowered by placing it on the ground for three days, exposing it to the Sun and Moon for three days, and by placing it in a tree for three days, for a total of nine days. To use the staff, point it toward a magical focus such as a crystal, a ritual fire, or the statue of a deity with whom you work, and envision your intent flowing out to the world. Experienced practitioners will be able to harness the energy of any powerful natural feature—like a river, the Sun, or the Moon and use it to send intent with a wand or staff.

Archaeologists recently announced finding a 4,400-year-old wooden stick carved into the shape of a snake near a lake in southwest Finland. They conclude that it was probably used for mystical purposes by a shaman. The reasearchers noted, "The figure, which is 21 inches (53 centimeters) long and about an inch (2.5 centimeters) thick, was carved from a single piece of wood. . . . The figurine is very naturalistic and resembles a grass snake (*Natrix natrix*) or a European adder (*Vipera berus*) in the act of slithering or swimming away."[1]

The Apple Branch

The Apple branch is so named because in Celtic lore a visitor from the Otherworld will arrive carrying a silver Apple branch with white Apple blossoms upon it. That's how you will know them. In the tales it is known as an *An Craobh Airgid* (the Silver Branch or Silver Bough).

The Apple branch, bell branch, or Silver Bough is a tool I always use to open a Druid rite. I have several I have made of wood over the years; one is natural wood with bells, and the other is painted silver with silver bells tied on with silver thread. When I travel, I like to bring a flexible and lightweight rope version that has many bells attached.

The sound of the bells is a signal to the Nature Spirits that a ritual is about to begin. They like the sound of tinkling bells as much as they love music.

I walk the ritual circle deiseal (sunwise) three times, shaking the bells, before anyone else enters the space or lights the fire.

Making an Apple Branch

First meditate and ask the Goddesses and Gods to show you which tree will donate its wood to you, and which tree is best suited to your own spiritual journey at this time. You can do this at home, or while walking in a forest. Keep doing this every day until you get a firm message.

Look for a recently fallen branch from the tree species you desire. If none can be found, then cut the end of a branch for your use (but this is a last resort). Going out after a big storm will often be the best time to find newly fallen wood.

Make sure to leave a gift for the tree from which you "bought" wood: a drink in a dry spell, an offering of herbs, fertilizer, cider, milk, honey, a few coins buried at its base, and so on. Tell the tree why you took its wood, and honor it with a song or a prayer for its health and well-being, and by burying a circle of crystals around it or by planting flower bulbs at its base. You could even hang a bird feeder from its branches, to give it company.

Next, tie nine bells (or multiples of nine) onto the branch. Then shake the Apple branch in celebration to please the Tree Spirit and the Fairies nearby.

The Druid Egg

There is also another kind of egg, of much renown in the Gallic provinces, but ignored by the Greeks. In the summer, numberless snakes entwine themselves into a ball, held together by a secretion from their bodies and by their spittle. This is called anguinum. The Druids say that hissing serpents throw this up into the air, and that it must be caught in a cloak, and not allowed to touch the ground; and that one must instantly take flight on horse-back, as the serpents will pursue until some stream cuts them out. It may be tested, they say, by seeing if it floats against the current of a river, even though it be set in gold. But as it is the way of magicians to cast a cunning veil about their frauds, they pretend that these eggs can only be taken on a certain day of the moon, as though it rested with mankind to make the moon and the serpents accord as to the moment of the operation. I myself, however, have seen one of these eggs; it was round, and about as large as a smallish apple; the shell was cartilaginous, and pocked like the arms of a polypus.

PLINY THE ELDER, *NATURAL HISTORY*, XXIX.52

In Wales these are known as *mân macal* (snare stones) and *glain y nidir* (the snake's jewel). The Druid's egg was so powerful a talisman that it could affect the outcome of a court case. The Romans even made carrying one into a courtroom illegal and punishable by death.[2]

No one is really sure what substance these ancient Eggs were made of; some say glass. For modern Druids the Druid egg is a quartz crystal egg used for magic and for scrying (divination by peering into the egg to perceive images).

In ancient European belief eggs were magical objects because the round orb of an egg was capable of transforming into a chicken. To effect magic with an egg you had to deprive it of chicken-hood. The energy that would have gone into transforming the gelatinous liquid inside the egg into bone, feathers, and blood, would instead be directed to empowering other transformations. Eggs were hidden in stores of grain to make them fruitful and buried in gardens to boost their health and output.

Drawings and symbols of what one desired were painted on an egg that was then buried in the ground. The drawings communicated wishes and intentions to the Spirits, and the energy of the egg would make the wishes come true.

Modern Druids work with chicken eggs, of course (for this kind of magic organic, fertile eggs must be used), but we also keep a Druid egg made of crystal for magical workings. Such an egg is used for scrying or placed in water that is drunk to increase the fertility of women and of projects.

Aquiring, Consecrating, and Using Your Druid Egg

You will likely need to purchase or barter for your Druid egg.

Once you have it, purify it by burying it in the Earth for three days, then by exposing it to the Sun and Moon for three days, and then by placing it in the hollow of a tree for three days—a total of nine days to energize it and awaken its powers.

Next you will consecrate the egg with fragrant smoke or an herbal bath, asking for the blessings of the protector Deities with whom you work.

The egg can then be stored in your crane bag along with other sacred talismans.

To scry with your Druid egg, hold it before a candle flame or in sunlight or moonlight while asking a question. Pay attention to what images appear in your mind's eye. A crystal egg with many imperfections is best for this, as more images will suggest themselves.

After each magical use the egg should be purified with smoke or an herbal brew, rinsed with clear running water, and be exposed to the rays of the Sun and Moon as a blessing.

The Sickle

The Druids—for that is the name they give to their magicians—held nothing more sacred than the mistletoe and the tree that bears it, supposing always that tree to be the robur. Of itself the robur is selected by them to form whole groves, and they perform none of their religious rites without employing branches of it; so much so, that it is very probable that the priests themselves may have received their name from the Greek name for that tree. In fact, it is the notion with them that everything that grows on it has been sent immediately from heaven, and that the mistletoe upon it is a proof that the tree has been selected by God himself as an object of his especial favour.

The mistletoe, however, is but rarely found upon the robur; and when found, is gathered with rites replete with religious awe. This is done more particularly on the fifth day of the moon, the day which is the beginning of their months and years, as also of their ages, which, with them, are but thirty years. This day they select because the moon, though not yet in the middle of her course, has already considerable power and influence; and they call her by a name which signifies, in their language, the all-healing. Having made all due preparation for the sacrifice and a banquet beneath the trees, they bring thither two white bulls, the horns of which are bound then for the first time. Clad in a white robe the priest ascends the tree, and cuts the mistletoe with a golden sickle, which is received by others in a white cloak. They then immolate the victims, offering up their prayers that God will render this gift of his propitious to those to whom he has so granted it. It is the belief with them that the mistletoe, taken in drink, will impart fecundity to all animals that are barren, and that it is an antidote for all poisons.

PLINY THE ELDER IN
NATURAL HISTORY, VOLUME XVI

The "robur" mentioned by Pliny is, of course, the Pedunculate Oak, European Oak, or English Oak (*Quercus robur*). Mistletoe does grow on other trees such as Apples and Poplars, but for medicinal use the *Viscum album* that grows on Oak is the very best to reduce tumors. I believe that the old Druids must have known that. **Please note that this is not a Mistletoe variety that grows in America. American varieties are poisonous.**

The "golden sickle" mentioned by Pliny could not have been made of gold, as that metal is too soft to cut herbs so it was most likely made of bronze. The golden sickle could also be a reference to the Moon. This rite is the only account of an actual Druid ritual that we have a record of, and it was performed at the New Moon, on the fifth day after the first appearance of the waxing Moon.

It is worth noting that, in the ritual, the Druids wear white and hold a white cloth to catch the Mistletoe. Mistletoe has white berries, and such robes could have been worn just for this specific rite, to honor the plant. Modern Druids often choose to sport long, white robes when doing a ceremony, possibly to better distinguish themselves from Witches, who generally wear black. I have been a Druid for many years, and I can assure you that the ancient Druids most likely did not traipse around all day in pristine white robes that fell all the way to the ground. White clothing is notoriously difficult to keep clean, and we do know from other accounts that Druids wore many colors of clothing as well as feathered capes. If they did wear white, I am willing to bet that their tunics hung well above the dirt and grime, as in figure 22 (see below) of the Genii Cucullati, or Hooded Spirits, and other similar figures found in religious sculptures across the Romano-Celtic regions.

I have two sickles; a small handmade one crafted by the Druid smith Justin Fisher, which he gave to me as a gift, and a larger one that I found at a hardware store and painted with bronze-colored paint to conform to Pliny's description. I fashioned a leather covering for the

Figure 22. Relief of the Genii Cucullati (Hooded Spirits).
Found in a shrine in the vicus, in early third century CE. Image shared by Carole Raddato, CC BY-SA 2.0/Wikimedia Commons.

smaller sickle, so the blade won't accidentally stab me when I hang it on my belt. One should only use a Druid sickle for the cutting of ceremonial herbs, and not for other mundane purposes.

There is a type of divination that can be done if you are lucky enough to have three or more consecrated sickles or attend a gathering where several Druids possess a sickle. Hold the three sickles in your hand and swing them in a circle deiseal three times above your head and then let the sickles fly (be very attentive as to who is around you—the last thing you want is for a fellow Druid to become a human sacrifice!).

Where the sickles land will give you your divination: North for fire, battle, the sword, and the Eagle; East for earth, abundance, Salmon and Bee; South for water, music, poetry, song, Boar, and Sow; West for air, history keeping, genealogy, and Stag; the Sacred Center for mastery, rulership, and the great Mare of Sovereignty.

As with all magical tools, keep your sickle covered in cloth or in a leather bag when not in use. And after each magical working it should be purified with smoke, rinsed with clear running water, and be exposed to the rays of the Sun and Moon as a blessing.

Druidic Meditation

Three excellences of wisdom: to be aware of all things, to
suffer with all things, and to be detached from all things.
ANCIENT IRISH TRIAD

The first time I visited Ireland I sat on the bank of the river Boyne and meditated. I did what I always do when I meditate in nature: I got into a lotus position with crossed knees, grounded, centered, and softened my eyes, leaving them slightly open. Suddenly there was a great commotion on the surface of the water. Huge fish were leaping as if in greeting, right in front of me! I felt I was being welcomed personally by the sacred salmon of the Boyne. I had no idea that there is a great salmon run on the Boyne in early autumn, and I must have been there at exactly the right time.

At one point a kingfisher soared past and then perched on a branch nearby. Kingfishers dive deep into the depths to gather their sustenance. As an animal Spirit, kingfisher urges us to reach for the deep unknown, even if the waters are murky. It encourages us to overcome our fears and to plunge fearlessly into something new. I was just at the beginning of my Celtic Druid studies. These kinds of signs and portents often crop up when I take the time to be still and listen.

Meditation not only allows a Druid to achieve mental peace and bodily health, it allows us to slow down and open ourselves to nature. For this reason, every Druid should learn at least one meditation technique such as Zen Meditation, Transcendental Meditation, Vipassana, or Mindfulness. While the ancient Druids once practiced forms of meditation such as the Stone on the Belly Technique (see page 133), many modern methods or ancient methods from other parts of the world are easily available to be learned today.

Meditation is also how we activate what I call our Salmon Wisdom. Salmon is a sacred animal of the Celts, associated with prosperity and the eastern direction. Salmon are spawned in a clear stream and unerringly find their way to the great salt ocean. Then they wander the seas for two years, and at the right time magically return to the exact stream of their birth because they know how to get back to Source. Similarly, in deep meditation a Druid can ask a question and then allow their thoughts to bubble up peacefully, like the waters of the Well of Segais, the Well of Wisdom, which is the source of the river Boyne. The Boyne is sacred to the Goddess Boann, She of the White Cow and of the Way of the White Cow (the Milky Way).

Nine sacred Hazels of Wisdom surround the Well of Wisdom, which bloom and give fruit at the same time. As the hazelnuts fall into the Well, they are eaten by the salmon who gain a spot for every hazelnut consumed. Eating the hazelnuts that fall into the Well, drinking the Well's water, or eating the salmon that eat the hazelnuts is said to grant knowledge and poetic inspiration. It is possible that the spots on the salmon once represented poetic grades or Druidic achievements.

In modern times scientists find answers by external hypothesis and experiment. In ancient times sages went into deep meditation, diving within to divine conclusions, following a question to the Source, and allowing the answer to bubble up from the depths of consciousness.

There are many kinds of meditation you can learn. Some involve sitting, others are associated with Yogic postures. Even walking mindfully in the woods can be a form of meditation. Tread carefully and be conscious of every step and breath as you move through the forest. Hear the birds and the wind soughing through the trees. Stay centered, and any time your thoughts wander off just bring them gently back and continue on your way. Gwennic, a Tribe of the Oak Druid, had this to say about his meditative experience:

> Personally, meditation has been a part of my work as a walker between the worlds. I was taught by the trees themselves that sitting and listening and waiting for answers was vital. As one who works with divination and on an oracle path, meditation has been my saving grace many times, allowing the visions and the spirits to flow to me and act as a conduit of knowledge for others. Meditation has helped me to see that checking my own ego is essential, and helps bring more curiosity, patience, and love into my life.

Learning to meditate is the fundamental basis for Seership, scrying, and trance work and a way to directly contact the ancestors and Spirits. It is also vital to our mental and physical health. According to the Mayo Clinic, meditation brings the following benefits:

> Gaining a new perspective on stressful situations.
> Increasing self-awareness.
> Focusing on the present.
> Reducing negative emotions.
> Increasing imagination and creativity.
> Increasing patience and tolerance.

The Mayo Clinic notes that research suggests meditation may help ease the following health conditions:[1]

Anxiety	Heart disease
Asthma	High blood pressure
Cancer	Irritable bowel syndrome
Chronic pain	Sleep problems
Depression	Tension headaches

As you can now appreciate, meditation brings us many benefits and gifts; better health, mental peace, a deeper connection to nature, and a technique to find answers to the mysteries of life.

Using Meditation to Ground for Ritual

Three essentials of poetic genius: an eye to see nature, a heart to feel nature, and a resolute courage that dares to follow nature.

ANCIENT IRISH TRIAD

Grounding is an essential skill of the Druid. It is important to do it before a ritual and before a meditative walk in the forest. I always do it before performing either of the three cauldrons meditations below.

If for some reason you need to ground quickly, just become aware of your feet and your breathing, soften your knees (unlock them), and send your energy down through your legs to the soles of your feet and to the ground beneath you. Do this until you feel very balanced and solid, almost like a surfer on her board, getting ready for a wave. Then notice how the Earth is supporting you and holding you up.

This technique is useful when you begin a magical working and even when you have high blood pressure or have received shocking news. It will help you to focus and to "Keep calm and carry on."

The Three Cauldrons Meditations

Three foundations of learning: seeing much, studying much, and suffering much.

ANCIENT IRISH TRIAD

"The Cauldron of Poesy" is a seventh-century Old Irish poem that refers to three "cauldrons" that every person is born with. Below is a section from Erynn Rowan Laurie's translation:

What then is the root of poetry and every other wisdom? Not hard; three cauldrons are born in every person—the cauldron of warming, the cauldron of motion and the cauldron of wisdom.

The **cauldron of warming** is born upright in people from the beginning. It distributes wisdom to people in their youth.

The **cauldron of motion**, however, increases after turning; that is to say it is born tipped on its side, growing within.

The **cauldron of wisdom** is born on its lips and distributes wisdom in poetry and every other art.[2]

I equate these cauldrons with the chakra system because in ancient Sanskrit writings there were many different numbers of chakra systems—but three were especially significant, as Tantra scholar Christopher D. Wallis highlights:

. . . there are a few centers which are found in all systems: specifically, in the lower belly or sexual center, in the heart, and in or near the crown of the head, since these are three places in the body where humans all over the world experience both emotional and spiritual phenomena.[3]

It seems entirely possible that the three predominant chakras in both Hindu scriptures and in Druidic poetry derive from the same proto-Vedic source.

The three Celtic cauldrons are named Coire Goiriath (the cauldron of warming, sustenance, or incubation), Coire Ernmae (the cauldron of motion, arts, or vocation), and Coire Sois (the cauldron of inspiration, wisdom, or knowledge).

The cauldron of warming is found in the abdomen. This is a wheel of energy that governs basic survival such as metabolism, sex, keeping the body warm, and digesting food. It is upright in everyone at their birth, turns on its side during sickness, and turns upside down in death.

The cauldron of motion is in the area of the heart. In most people it is on its side, but extremes of joy and sorrow can turn it upright, thereby making it a vessel for the poetic arts.

The cauldron of wisdom is in the head. It is upside down in most people but can be turned upright by poetic training and by the intervention of the Goddesses and Gods.

Once the cauldrons are turned fully upright, they become receptacles to receive and contain divine inspiration, and the recipient attains immortal abilities.

As one example of the turning cauldrons, anyone who is an artist, such as a painter, musician, or poet will have noticed the energy that builds in their chest when passionate streams of creativity are flowing. You may also have noticed how dead this area feels after a shocking experience or a great loss.

A Three Cauldrons Meditation
Using the Three Cauldrons to Solve Problems and Understand Situations

- First, pick a situation, person, place, or thing.
- Holding it in your mind, "pour" it through your Cauldron of Warming, which is in your belly about two fingers below your navel. Your Cauldron of Warming (in your gut) will sense things about an object that the Cauldron of Motion (in your chest) will miss. It will approach the object from a practical standpoint.
- Now focus on the Cauldron of Motion that resides in the chest, near your heart area. Think about the person, place, thing, or situation you are contemplating. The Cauldron of Motion will see the object in an emotional, poetic, and artistic light.
- Now bring your awareness to your Third Eye (the point between and slightly above your eyebrows) and run the same objects or issues through your perception there. Your Cauldron of Wisdom will think about the object, its past, present, and future implications, and give you additional insights.

I also find meditating on the three cauldrons to be supremely useful in communicating with trees, stones, plants, fire, water, clouds, or any object that most people would consider to be inanimate (we Druids know better). It is a method of scrying into any aspect of nature whose wisdom you seek. Think of it as a type of full-body dowsing.

A Three Cauldrons Meditation
Using the Three Cauldrons to Communicate with Nature

- Begin by grounding (see the grounding technique on page 127)
- Then approach the tree, herb, rock, fire, or other nature element you are working with.
- Use all your senses to understand it.
- First see it with your eyes, then feel it with your fingers, inhale its fragrance, and listen to its leaves or other sounds.
- Sit very close to it or even embrace it, and then run it through your three cauldrons.
- Feel into your cauldrons and ask each energy center what the Spirit of the tree, mountain, herb, rock, stream, fire, or other nature element is saying.
- If you do get a message, be sure to reciprocate with a gift of thanks.

You can use this technique with animals, rivers, lakes, the ocean, a landscape, a star, the Moon, or any other natural feature you wish to explore.

The Tree Meditation

There are many different versions of this exercise floating around, and this is just one example. I have been doing it with groups and by myself for over thirty years. It's a wonderful technique to do as a prelude to the three cauldron meditations above, a spiritual walk in the forest, or a Druid ritual. You will feel slightly tranced out, and that's as it should be.

Tree Meditation

- Close your eyes or soften them until they are relaxed and only slightly open.
- Become aware of your feet and feel your connection to the soil (if you are inside, visualize the soil deep beneath the building you are in).
- Allow your knees to soften (unlock them) and bend slightly.
- Allow the weight of your body to sink like the contents of a sack of flour that has been picked up by the two top corners.
- Open the "eyes" at the bottom of your feet.
- "See" the ground beneath you and feel your toes start to grow longer as they burrow into the soil.
- Keep going down into the dirt and notice the streams of water, electrical currents, rocks, crystals, and creatures such as snakes, worms, and bugs that you pass on your way.
- Keep sending your roots down and down until they grow ever thinner.
- Keep going until your roots are just threads, and then go deeper still.
- Notice that your roots have become filaments of light.
- Send your light down until you become aware of a green pulsing glow and warmth coming from the very heart of the planet (this is known as the Emerald Heart of the Earth in some Fairy circles).
- Hook your light filaments into the Green Heart of the Earth and begin to move your awareness back up to your earthly roots.
- As your awareness rises upward again, notice the stones, crystals, streams of water and electrical currents, the bugs, worms, and snakes that you passed going down.
- Keeping your light filaments and roots firmly anchored at the center of the Earth, move your awareness slowly to the top of your head.
- Open the eye at the top of your head, your Crown Chakra, the part of your skull that was still soft when you were first born, and begin to send filaments of light up to the Sky Realm.
- When you reach the Sun (or the Moon, or even a star if it's night) anchor your filaments of light to the celestial orb.

- At this point you should be feeling very tall, stretched, and thin. You are now existing in the same realm as the trees and living between the Worlds.
- Leaving your filaments firmly attached to the Soil and Sun, become aware of your breathing and your heart.
- Begin a circular breath; inhale up from the Emerald Heart of the Earth, through your Heart Chakra, up through your head, and following your filaments of light, all the way to the Sun.
- Next exhale from the Sun down to your head and along your spine to your legs and roots and filaments of light, all the way to the center of the Earth.
- Inhale again from the center of the Earth to your heart and to the Sun, and exhale down from the Sun to your spine and to the Heart of the Earth. Repeat this circular breath nine times.
- We Druids say that we worship in Groves. By doing this breath everyone in your ritual circle has entered the Kingdom of the Trees, and they have become a true Grove. This is the work that living trees do every day and night, pulling up energy from the ground through their roots, collecting sunlight and dispersing it to the air and soil through their leaves and fruits.
- When your ritual is done, reverse the process.
- Open the eye at the top of your head and follow the light filaments to the Sun or other celestial light, unhook them, and bring everything back down to your head.
- Close the eye at the top of your head.
- Send your awareness down to your feet, open the eyes in the soles of your feet and follow the roots and filaments down to the Emerald Heart of the Earth and unhook them.
- Pull everything up through the layers of soil, stone, and water, back into your feet.
- Close the eyes in the bottom of your feet.
- Become aware of your breathing and your heartbeat.
- At the count of three or when you feel 100 percent human again, open your eyes fully and reenter the day-to-day world.
- If you still feel dizzy, find a tree to hug or lean against. Every tree knows how to channel excess energy, and it will realign your chakras.

Note: I like to say that no one should walk away from the ritual site after doing this exercise until they feel they are at least sixteen years old and capable of driving.

A Few Bardic Exercises

Here are a few bardic training exercises you can do, alone or with a group. The ancient Druids and Bards spent many years in study and these are just a few of the poetic exercises they practiced in their training. These types of practices were designed to spark imbas and poetic inspiration.

Stone on the Belly Technique

- If possible, practice this exercise after fasting for a while before you start. Fasting will make you more open to visions and inspiration.
- Shut all doors and windows to minimize sound, pulling the blinds or curtains to bring in the dark.
- Lie on your back on the floor with a large stone on your belly and a plaid wrapped around your head to block out all light.
- Begin by becoming aware of your emotions and stay in that position until you incubate a poem, using a specific rhyme scheme, meter, or alliteration.

Pursuing Salmon Wisdom

Salmon are born upstream in clear waters. They unerringly find their way to the salt sea, where they spend two years, then return effortlessly to the exact stream of their birth.

When you have a question or a problem to solve, instead of trying to think it through, go into meditation. Allow your thoughts to bubble up by themselves, and gently dismiss any thoughts that are not helpful. Pursue your question to the Source by allowing the answer to emerge on its own.

The Song of Amergin Exercise

- Lie down in a dark place with the door and windows shut and a plaid around your head to block out the light.
- Take just one line from the Amergin's song (see page 197), for example "I am a powerful ox," "I am a salmon in pools," or "I am a hawk on a cliff" and repeat it ninety-nine times (mala beads or prayer beads are helpful for this).
- Allow images, feelings, and the wisdom of the creature you invoked to take over and bring you on a shamanic journey.

Creating Druid Rituals

Three things from which never to be moved: one's Gods,
one's oaths and the truth

ANCIENT IRISH TRIAD

As a Druid you may be be called upon to perform seasonal rites, baby blessings, house blessings, handfastings, funerals, and other sacred observances. Every situation is unique, and you will need to use your imbas to devise rituals, props, readings, and invocations that are appropriate to each event and to the people involved.

Texts such as the *Rig Veda*, with its hymns to trees, fire, water, cows, horses, and the Sun, and the *Carmina Gadelica*, with its traditional Scottish prayers and invocations, will be invaluable for this work.

For private devotions a simple altar with a bowl of water, a candle, and a tree branch (symbolic of the Three Worlds) can suffice. For larger group rituals you will need to master a ritual form.

As Celtic Reconstructionists we always aim to use actual Celtic and Indo-European beliefs and practices in our rites. The approach below was honed over thirty years of practice both live and online with the Order of the White Oak, Tribe of the Oak, and several in person Druid Groves.

A Very Basic Druid Ritual Form

Here is a basic Celtic Druid ritual form. You will need to flesh it out as appropriate to the season and for other spiritual requirements. Ideally it should be done out of doors in a liminal space where Land, Sea (or any body of water), and Sky come together.

Offerings will be made to the Three Worlds: Land (Nature Spirits including plants, birds, animals, and trees), Sea (Sidhe Realm, Ancestors), and Sky (the Goddesses and Gods). Water carries your offerings down to the Underworld of the Ancestors and the Fairies, while fire carries your offerings up to the Sky World of the Goddesses and the Gods. Offerings strewn on the land belong to the Nature Spirits.

Seek out a place where there is living water—a stream or creek, lake, pond, deep well, waterfall, the ocean, or a river. You will need to build a fire and there should be a large tree nearby (on the beach you can use a staff to substitute for a tree). If you are lucky enough to have a large standing stone in your area it can substitute for a tree.

Be sure to check local weather reports and don't attempt a fire outdoors if there are wind, dry conditions, or brushfire danger. Consider building your fire in a metal fire bowl with legs, as that will prevent the earth from becoming scorched. Always have containers filled with water nearby, in case a spark escapes.

If you are confined to the indoors or fire risk in your area is high, a cauldron of water, a cauldron of fire (or candles inside a cauldron), and a small potted tree or a tree branch work well. After the rite someone will need to carry the water and its offerings to a source of living water, such as a river, and pour it in, and take the offerings for the Land and selectively place them outdoors.

The Steps for a Basic Druid Ritual

1. Ground and center. Meditate on tree imagery, visualizing your roots going down to the Earth and your branches (arms and head) stretching

to the Sky. (See instructions for Tree Meditation on page 131.)

2. Purify each person and all ritual tools with Sage, Juniper, Cedar, or any other sacred smoke or herbal wash.

3. Process to the ritual area, singing. Use your bell branch as a rhythm instrument as you dance and sing, because the Good Folk (Fairies) enjoy the sound.

4. One person should make an offering away from the ritual site to the Fomorians and any other mischievous Spirits that they be satisfied and stay away from the ceremony.

5. Announce the rite: explain to the congregation and to any listening Spirits why you have gathered and your purpose.

6. Invoke Manannán MacLir to open the veil between the worlds.

7. Make offerings to water (fresh fruits, flowers, silver coins, jewelry, or other things that won't pollute the water) and sing to it. Make offerings to the Ancestors and the Daoine Sidhe (DEENA-shee), or Good Neighbors (Fairies), who help the crops to grow and enliven the living land and sing to them. If possible, circumambulate the water source three times, singing.

8. Make offerings to a tree, such as herbs, flowers, fruits, compost, mushrooms, water if the land is dry, or anything a tree might enjoy, invoking the Land Spirits and giving them thanks. Dance around the tree three times, singing. Remember that trees span all three Worlds—they have roots that go down to the Sidhe Realm and branches that reach up to the Sky Goddesses and Gods.

9. Light the fire and make offerings to fire, such as dried herbs, scented woods, oil, whiskey, butter, or ghee (things that fire likes); circumambulate the fire three times, singing.

10. At this point you may wish to call in the Five Directions. This will look and sound different from the Wiccan form that most neo-Pagans are used to. In Celtic thinking Salmon is in the East, the direction of earth and abundance; Boar/Sow is in the South, the direction of water, poetry, and song; Stag is in the West, the direction of air and of history keeping; and Eagle is in the North, the direction of battle and of fire. In the Sacred Center stands the Great Mare of Sovereignty, in the direction of mastery.

Note: if you are alone in the forest, you can set up a simple ritual area with just five stones or five acorns!

11. Invoke the deities of the occasion, and then make offerings to them of songs, music, or poetry. Read or recite a story about them, or make a sacrificial offering of artwork, crafts, foods, or the like, which are burned in the fire, to send them to the Sky Realm.

12. Now you can make your petition to the Goddesses and Gods if you have a request, or perform a specific ritual as indicated by need (such as a seasonal observance, funeral, or handfasting).

13. Do a divination to see if the Goddesses and Gods have accepted the rite/request. A very simple way to do that is to stand silently and wait for a sign. If a large bird flies overhead, or an Oak leaf or branch falls at your feet, there is sudden wind or thunder, or the fire pops loudly, for example, those are very good signs. If the fire suddenly dies or a cloud appears out of nowhere and drenches you (unless you have petitioned for rain!), it may be a warning that the rite needs more energy. In that case make more offerings, sing more loudly, pray harder, or make an oath to do a service for the people and the Goddesses and Gods, and then do another divination to see if the rite was accepted.

14. Another way to determine if the rite was approved by the Goddesses, Gods, and Spirits is to use Ogham fews (Ogham letters), or any other divination technique, and have a Seer read the signs.

15. When you are sure the rite has been accepted, give thanks to the Goddesses and Gods of the occasion.

16. Give thanks to the Salmon, Boar/Sow, Stag, Eagle, and the Great Mare for their help.

17. Give thanks to the fire.

18. Give thanks to the Good Neighbors for their presence.

19. Give thanks to the trees and the Nature Spirits.

20. Give thanks to the waters, the Ancestors, and the Sidhe.

21. Ask Manannán MacLir to close the veil.

22. Process back home, singing.

23. Have a feast!

A Sample Lughnasad Ritual

You will, of course, write your own words for your rites. Here are some suggestions from a Lughnasad ritual that was done by Tribe of the Oak in 2021, online, during the Covid pandemic. Everyone was asked to make offerings to the Land Spirits in their own area before the ritual began, and during the rite we each had fragrant herbs to smudge ourselves and a candle to light. One nice thing about doing rituals online is that you can find wonderful selections of Celtic music to play in the background and persons from different countries can gather to do ceremony at the same time!

Opening the Gates between the Worlds
Petitioning Manannán MacLir

Oh God of Sea, Manannán MacLir, be with us now!
Part the veil so that we may
Commune with the Wise Ones.
Open the watery veil,
To the Spirits' domain,
And sail them to us
From across the waves.

Calling In the Three Worlds
Making Offerings to the Spirits of the Land,
to Sacred Water, to Fire, and to Trees

We invoke the sacred three: Land, Sea, and Sky!

Ancestors, you whose blood and bone have made the soil upon which we stand, Ancestors of our bloodlines whose sacrifice of love and tears have enabled us to be alive today, Ancestors of our Spirit whose teachings have been bequeathed to us in books and schools and in our listening, we honor you, and we welcome you into our circle!

*Nature Spirits, seen and unseen, you who have given your flesh,
blood, and fur so that we may eat and live. You who have given
us your love, we welcome you here—winged, scaley, furred, and
feathered ones and the trees and herbs of the forests and fields.
The Elementals who make our gardens grow and the Little
People who help us with our work. Please be with us in
our circle. We thank you, and we honor your presence here!*

*All the Goddesses and Gods of our people, known and unknown,
named and unnamed, you whose wisdom and care have guided us
through the seasons of our lives. Be with us here in our circle!
We honor you and ask for your blessings!*

∞

Calling in the Five Directions

*Salmon of the East! Bringer of abundance! Welcome to our circle.
Bestow upon us prosperity, fat cattle, and hives rich with honey.
May we have beautiful raiment, warm firesides, and delicious food!
Spirit of the Realm of Earth—bless us with fertility and wealth.
Welcome Sacred Salmon!*

*Great Sow of the South! You who delve deep into the dark to bring up
truth and inspiration, bless us with your presence! Bring us your gifts
of poetry, song, and music. We honor you and your creativity.
From the deep realms of water, we welcome
you into our circle. Be with us now!*

*Sacred Stag of the West! Guardian of air and of history, storytelling,
and genealogy! Be with us in this sacred space! We honor your
wisdom and determination. Show us a good direction! Help
us to persevere in our learning, teaching, and studies.
Great Stag, be with us now!*

*Fire Eagle of the North! Keeper of the Sword of Light. Lord of
Battle and Defender of the Realms, be with us now!
Teach us to be fearless. Teach us to protect the*

ancient ways of the tribes. Help us to be a shield for the people.
Great Eagle from the realm of sacred fire, be with us now!

Great Mare of Sovereignty! You who stand in the center of all that is,
seeing all, from every direction, be with us here in our circle. Teach us
self-mastery. Keep us centered on our path. Help us to do what is right
for all lives! We welcome you here. Be with us now!

ⓖↄ

Invoking the God*

Invocation of Lugh

Thou Lugh the victorious,
We make our circuit under thy shield,
Thou Lugh of the white steed,
And of the bright brilliant blades,
Conqueror of the dragon,
Be thou at our backs,
Thou ranger of the heavens,
Thou warrior for us all.
On the meadows,
On the cold heathery hills,
Though we should travel the oceans
And the hard globe of the world
No harm can e'er befall us
'Neath the shelter of thy shield.
Peace is with us;
With our horses, with our cattle,
With our woolly sheep in flocks.
With our crops growing in the field,
Or ripening in the sheaf.
On the moor, in heaps and stacks.
Everything on high or low,

---

*These invocations were inspired by the *Carmina Gadelica*.

Every furnishing and flock,
Is under thy protection.

༄

Invoking the Goddess
Honoring of Tailtiu

Great-hearted Tailtiu,
Daughter of kings,
Beloved bride of Eochaid
Enduring one who lived through sorrow
And loss.
You who weathered the storms of war
And stood strong despite hardships.
Foster-mother of many-skilled Lugh
Kind one who cared well for the long-armed one,
The clever, crafty one,
As if he were your own dear child.
In gratitude for your love and safe-keeping
In honor of your goodness and your mettle
Did he decree that games be held,
That all should feast and compete in sport and arts
In your name,
Recalling your virtues and your great worth.

༄

Petitions for Healing and Assistance

Lugh and Tailtiu, we have honored you at this gathering.
We have placed our offerings into the fire and into
our sacred well, in your name. Please hear us now.

At this point people can speak their need out loud, inscribe it
on paper or on Birch bark and place it in the fire, or just silently
send up a request.

汐汐

Divination

Our Seer will now seek the will of the Goddesses
and Gods and perform a divination.

The seer uses cards, bones, stones, Ogham fews, or any other divinatory method of their choosing. The Seer gives a reading to the assembly. When the Seer is finished, resume with the below.

The Goddesses and Gods have spoken!
Thank you, Lugh and Tailtiu!

汐汐

Thanking the Directions

Great Salmon of the East! Thank you for gracing us with your
presence here. May your journey through the seas be swift and sure.
Hail and farewell!

Great Sow of the South. Thank you for your gifts to us of music and
song. Long may you delve the dark places to bring forth creativity!
Hail and farewell!

Great Stag of the West! Thank you for keeping our learning alive.
Thank you for inspiring our studies.
Hail and farewell!

Fire Eagle of the North! Thank you for giving us courage,
determination, and certitude. Thank you for your strength!
Hail and farewell!

Beloved Mare of Sovereignty! Thank you for keeping us centered like a
mighty Oak. Thank you for making us kings and queens within our
own realms. Thank you for the gift of mastery.
Hail and farewell!

Thanking the Goddesses and Gods

Thank you to the Goddesses and Gods of our people, the known and the unknown. You who have guided and protected us through the generations! Thank you for your presence here. Hail and Farewell!

Thanks to the Three Worlds: Land, Sea, and Sky

We send thanks to the Three Realms, to the Sacred Land, to the Realm of Sea and to the Sky! Thank you for giving us a place to dwell within the Worlds. Hail and Farewell!

Thanks to the Nature Spirits

All thanks to the Nature Spirits: the furry, finny, scaley, creepy, crawly, and winged ones. Thank you also to the unseen, hidden ones. Thank you for feeding us, for your beauty, for your love. Hail and Farewell!

Thanks to the Ancestors and the Sidhe

Thank you, Ancestors and Good Neighbors, for being with us once again in our circle. Thank you for your ceaseless toil and care and the wisdom to survive so we could all be here today. Hail and farewell!

Thanks to Manannán MacLir

O great God of the Headlands
And Son of the Sea,
Mighty Manannán MacLir,
We thank you for your help here today!
Please close the veil so that only the good may remain;
Only the highest and best for the people.

O Manannán, please close the portal now
And sail us safely home!

⟳

Ending the Rite

Thus ends our rite!
Thank you all for your presence here,
Safe travels and safe home!
Until the wheel turns once more,
Stay safe and be well!

After the rite it is traditional to have a feast. All participants should contribute seasonal foods and drink, to the best of their ability.

Druidic Rites for Special Life Passages

Here are some brief thumbnail sketches of Druidic rites for special life passages. You should feel free to change them and add or subtract elements as you see fit.

⟳

A Druidic Funeral Observance

Ask Manannán to part the veil then make the usual blessing of the ritual space, calling of directions, and offerings to water, fire, and trees. Make offerings and invitations to the Ancestors, Nature Spirits, and Goddesses and Gods.

Have an interlude of live harp music if possible.

Provide the opportunity to share memories of the person and their life for those who wish to speak. Optionally, some personal items belonging to the deceased may be shared out among friends and family.

Consecrate and share the waters of life (an alcoholic beverage or juice) and freshly made bread.

Compose a prayer along these lines:

As the ancient Druids have told us, death is but an interval in the midst of a long life. May the Nature Spirits guide [name] home, may the Honored Dead welcome [him/her] among them, may the High Ones grant [her/him] rest, and rebirth in due time. As it was, as it is, as it will be. There will be a returning for [name].

Have an interlude of harp (or other) music for reflection.

Consider placing sacred items such as a sword, a sickle, sacred herbs, a torc, or any other ritual tools used by the deceased into the casket, if there is one.

Build a cairn of stones over the body if it's a green burial, or over the casket or urn, if allowed.

Follow with feasting and funeral games (optional) if space permits.

෧౨

Handfasting Rite

Begin by asking Manannán to part the veil, calling in the directions, making offerings to water, fire, and trees, invoking the Ancestors, Nature Spirits, and Goddesses and Gods, and so on as above.

Next the couple can offer vows to one another (here we use bride and groom but substitute as fits the couple).

> **Groom:** [Name], *do you consent to be my wife?*

> **Bride:** *I do. Do you,* [name], *consent to be my husband?*

> **Groom:** *I do.*

Groom places a ring on the bride's finger

> **Groom:** *I take you as my wife, and I give myself*
> *to you as your husband.*

Bride places a ring on the groom's finger.

> **Bride:** *I take you as my husband, and I give myself to you as your wife.*

> **Groom:** *I, [name], now take you, [name], to be my wife. In the presence of the Ancestors, Nature Spirits, and Goddesses and Gods, and before these witnesses, I promise to be a loving, faithful, and loyal husband to you, for as long as we both shall live.*

> **Bride:** *I, [name], now take you, [name], to be my husband. In the presence of the Ancestors, Nature Spirits, and Goddesses and Gods, and before these witnesses, I promise to be a loving, faithful, and loyal wife to you, for as long as we both shall live.*

The officiant wraps a soft, woven belt around the hands of the couple. The couple can light three candles by holding one beeswax candle together with their free hands, touching it to the fire altar until it lights, and then together lighting two more candles, symbolic of their new life within the Three Worlds.

Give thanks to the Ancestors, Nature Spirits, and Goddesses and Gods, and to Manannán for opening the veil.

The couple departs to a private place to consummate their union. The three candles are left to blaze on the altar or may be placed at the high table where the couple will sit.

The other participants prepare a feast, organize music and dancing, and wait for the couple to reappear.

☌

In another variation there is a very old Scottish handfasting tradition where the couple sit on opposite sides of a stream and clasp hands underwater. Water is the gateway to the Ancestor's Realm, so by doing this they are pledging their troth in the sight of their forebears.

Rite of Childbirth

Before the baby is born the midwife or a family member shall consecrate the birth with sacred smoke and other offerings, a cauldron of water or a sacred well, and a fire altar kindled with nine sacred woods or of only Oak, and a Bíle (staff or sacred tree).

The Fire Altar

The fire in the fire altar shall be lit by the Sun focused through a crystal, by a "thunderstone" (flint), by a fire drill (using powdered Mistletoe as tinder), or from wildfire gathered from a lightning strike. The fire thus kindled shall be known as sacred fire.

The officiant shall circle the fire altar sunwise (clockwise) three times offering ghee, oil, or butter to the flames saying:

Brighid! Great Goddess of healing and inspiration, spread your cloak of protection around [name of the mother] *as she enters her time of travail. Spread your cloak also upon the little one who prepares to travel from one world to the next.*

The Sacred Cauldron

The officiant then moves to the cauldron or well and pours water into it from other sacred wells. It may also be water gathered during a thunderstorm, consecrated by a full Moon or by the Sun on a Holy Day (one of the four fire festivals), or sea water gathered from the ninth wave. Water thus gathered shall be known as sacred water.

The officiant circles the cauldron three times, pouring sacred water into it and visualizing the passage from one existence to the next, from one Ocean of Being to another, from Life to Life and saying:

Like a half Moon [baby's name if known or this baby] *is now outside of one world and not yet in the next, a Spirit moving from one existence to another. Make* [name or this baby's] *passage smooth, O Manannán. Make* [name or this baby's] *way easy as they die to the Otherworld. Open wide the gates of this world to* [name or this baby] *that we may soon see their face. Blessed Manannán make it so!*

The Sacred Tree*

The officiant shall address a sacred tree (or a staff planted ceremonially to represent a Bíle) saying:

Sister tree! Spirit who moves between the worlds with ease, from the above to the below, from the below to the above, root to branch and branch to root, guide this child as they move from one World to the next. Send them strength and fortify their life.

Rite of Baby Blessing

When the child emerges from the womb and the cord has been safely tied or at any time after the birth when a gathering can be assembled, the midwife, mother, or a relative shall take the child and hold it over the fire altar, passing it over the fire to a parent or a grandparent who shall pass it back three times saying:

May you be blessed all your days by holy fire and by the shining Sun.

Then the parent or grandparent shall walk three times sunwise around the fire altar carrying the child.†

The midwife, mother, father, or another relative shall then carry the child to the sacred cauldron or to a bath into which a silver coin has been placed. He or she shall gently wash the child by pouring nine wavelets of water upon it saying:

---

*It is worth noting that in ancient times women would hug a tree to promote fertility. An old method of childbirth was to cling to a branch while standing so that gravity would help bring the child down and out of the womb.

†When I performed this ritual in Ireland the baby was passed to each member of the extended family who were standing in a circle around the fire. As each person took the child, they spoke a blessing for the child and then handed it on to the next person, sunwise.

In the name of Brighid and of Manannán, nine blessings of water upon you. A blessing on your form that it be strong and beautiful to behold, a blessing on your voice that it be melodious, a blessing on your speech that it be eloquent, a blessing on your means that you may never want, a blessing on your generosity that you be always hospitable, a blessing on your appetite that it always be hale, a blessing on your wealth that you be prosperous, a blessing on your life that it be long, a blessing on your health that it be constant.

Then three drops shall be placed on the child's brow saying:

No seed of Fairy nor airy host nor human foe may best you. No evil eye nor envy nor malice disturb thy sleep or thy waking. May the loving arms of Brighid surround you and shield you this night and day, and every other day and night.

Other deities may be invoked, of course, if the parents so wish.

After the Birth

After the birth the placenta can be offered to a tree and the cord be buried beneath it or wrapped around its branches. This tree will ever after hold special significance for the child and for its family so the selection of such a tree should be done with care.

Charms and Hymns to the Sun and Moon

Three kinds of knowledge: the nature of each thing, the cause of each thing, the influence of each thing.

ANCIENT IRISH TRIAD

Druids usually do rituals outside in the sunlight, which makes our rites look and feel different from those of Witches, who tend to gather in the dark. But as Druids we may also have reasons to circle at night; for example, if there is an important celestial occurrence like an eclipse of the Moon. Such events always bring an alteration in the way things are going, and it's worthwhile to stop and take notice of the changes.

As Druids we can use the energy of the New Moon to begin a project, and recall that the famous Mistletoe-gathering rite that Pliny wrote about was done at the fifth day of the Moon (the fifth day after the appearance of the New Moon). We invoke changes and new beginnings at the New Moon, and banish or let go of things at the Waning Moon as in these examples from *Carmina Gadelica*.

Queen of the Night

Hail unto thee,
*   Jewel of the night!*
Beauty of the heavens,
*   Jewel of the night!*
Mother of the stars,
*   Jewel of the night!*
Fosterling of the sun,
*   Jewel of the night!*
Majesty of the stars,
*   Jewel of the night!*[1]

New Moon

When I see the new moon,
*   It becomes me to lift mine eye,*
*   It becomes me to bend my knee,*
*   It becomes me to bow my head.*

Giving thee praise, thou moon of guidance,
*   That I have seen thee again,*
*   That I have seen the new moon,*
*   The lovely leader of the way.*

Many a one has passed beyond
In the time between the two moons,
Though I am still enjoying the earth,
thou moon of moons and of blessings![2]

More often Druids will have reason to address the Sun as we do our ceremonies. Here are some examples of hymns of praise to our closest star. The first is from *Carmina Gadelica*.

The Sun

Hail to thee, thou sun of the seasons,
As thou traversest the skies aloft;
Thy steps are strong on the wing of the heavens,
Thou art the glorious mother of the stars.

Thou liest down in the destructive ocean
Without impairment and without fear;
Thou risest up on the peaceful wave-crest
Like a queenly maiden in bloom.[3]

These next brief excerpts come from a hymn in the *Rig Veda* addressing the driver of the Vedic Sun chariot, Agni, who is called Knower of Creatures and the Eye of the Gods. His chariot is pulled by seven mares or rays of light.

The Sun, Surya

. . . Crossing space, you are the maker of light seen by
everyone, O sun. You illumine the whole, wide realm of
space.
You rise up facing all the groups of gods, facing mankind,
facing everyone, so that they can see the sunlight . . .

You cross heaven and the vast realm of space, O sun,
    measuring days by nights, looking upon the generations.
Seven bay mares carry you in the chariot, O sun god with
    hair of flame, gazing from afar.
As you rise today, O sun, you who are honored as a friend,
    climbing to the highest sky, make me free of heartache
    and (yellow*) pallor.[4]

This quote is about the beautiful Sanskrit Goddess Savitri (Ray of Light, Daughter of the Sun):

Savitri,
love for the sun; a female creator (mother);
a ray of light (daughter of the sun);
conjugal love conquering death (from the ancient
    epic legend Mahabharata);
a vibrant link between earth and heaven (from
    Sri Aurobindo's poem Savitri);
incarnation (Goddess) of supreme truth;
the light which touches all;
love.[5]

Invoke changes and new beginnings by facing East at dawn, as the Sun rises. Banish or let go of things by facing West as the Sun goes down.

---

*Yellow pallor refers to jaundice—apparently the Vedic physicians knew that sunlight was a cure.

Charms for Divination and Augury

Three things avoided by the wise: expecting the impossible, grieving over the irretrievable, and fearing the inevitable

ANCIENT IRISH TRIAD

Every Druid needs to hone and perfect their divinatory skills. Pay attention to "day signs": animals that cross your path, celestial events, even numbers on license plates and stickers on cars. As an example, for me a flock of black birds always means a good day and prosperity. You will also want to perfect your knowledge of the ancient Irish Ogham (Ogam in Old Irish) alphabet (see below).

Here is a nice charm adapted from *Carmina Gadelica* to sing or recite as you begin a divination. In the place of "Mary" I have substituted the Morrígan and in place of "God" I have substituted "Gods" (plural) as well as a few other slight wording adjustments.

Augury Charm

*Goddesses and Gods over me, Goddesses and Gods
    under me,
Gods and Goddesses before me, Gods and Goddesses
    behind me,
I am on your path, O Goddesses and Gods of life,
    and you are in my steps.*

The augury Morrigan made at the battles end,
The offering made of Bride through her palm,
Did the Spirits witness it?—
    The Spirits did witness it.

The augury made by Morrigan about her people,
When the battle ended peace was made,
Knowledge of truth, not knowledge of falsehood,
    That I shall truly see all my quest.

Kindly spirits and Gods and Goddesses of life,
May you give me eyes to see all I seek,
With sight that shall never fail, before me,
    That shall never quench nor dim.[1]

These are examples from the *Carmina Gadelica* of the kinds of omens a Seer would look for:

Omens

Early on the morning of Monday,
I heard the bleating of a lamb,

And the kid-like cry of snipe.
While gently sitting bent,

And the gray-blue cuckoo.
And no food on my stomach.

On the fair evening of Tuesday,
I saw on the smooth stone,
The snail slimy, pale.

And the ashy wheatear*
On the top of the dyke of holes.

The foal of the old mare
Of sprauchly† gait and its back to me.

And I knew from these
That the year would not go well with me.[2]

I have adapted this verse, originally "Early Easter Monday," for a more Druidic tone.

Early on a Monday in the spring,
I saw on the brine
A duck and a white swan
    Swim together.

I heard on Tuesday
The snipe of the seasons,
Bleating on high
    And calling.

On Wednesday I had been
Outside gathering herbs,
And then saw I the three
    Arising.

I knew immediately
That there would not be,
    Blessing after that.

---

*A thrush
†Clumsy, ungainly

The blessings of Brighid calm,
The blessings of Danu mild,
The blessings of Lugh the strong,
Upon me and mine,
Upon me and mine.[3]

Divination by the Winds

Another form of divination involves assessing the direction of the prevailing wind. When setting out on a journey, at midnight on New Year's Eve, on any of the fire festivals, during eclipses, or other such occasions you can wet a finger and see which way things are about to go:

This list outlines the qualities of the different winds:

East Wind (*gaoth an ear*): Its color is purple (*corcur*) a color that implies nobility (because only nobles were allowed to wear the color purple) and art.

East Southeast Wind (*gaoth an ear ear-dheas*): Its color is yellow (*buidhe*) and it is a good wind for fruit, fish, and corn.

South Southeast Wind (*gaoth a deas ear-dheas*): Its color is red (*dearg*) and it is a good wind for fishing, luck, and prosperity.

South Wind (*gaoth a deas*): Its color is white (*geal*) and it brings a rich harvest.

South Southwest Wind (*gaoth a deas iar-dheas*): Its color is pallid or gray-green (*glas*). It brings blight, battle, and poor harvests.

West Southwest Wind (*gaoth an iar iar-dheas*): Its color is green (*uaine*) and it brings healing. It is the wind of the Mothers.

West Wind (*gaoth an iar*): Its color is dun, tan, or pale (*odhar*), and it brings the death of a king, bloodshed, and justice.

West North West Wind (*gaoth an iar iar-thuath*): Its color is gray (*liath*) and it brings death, slaughter, and the fall of blossoms.

North Northwest Wind (*gaoth an iar-thuath*): Its color is dusky, swarthy, gloomy sable (*ciar*) and it brings grumbling, quarrels, and sternness but also strength and vindication. It can sweep away disease.

North Wind (*gaoth a tuath*): Its color is black (*dubh*) and it brings battle magic and drought.

North Northeast Wind (*gaoth a tuath ear-thuath*): Its color is dark gray (*teimheil*) and it brings sickness and battle venom.

East Northeast Wind (*gaoth an ear ear-thuath*): Its color is speckled (*aladh*) and it brings enchantments and magic.

No wind: No wind at all is unheard of in the Scottish tradition, though I have been told that a calm wind means a peaceful outcome.*

Using Ogham for Divination

The Ogham alphabet most likely originated as a type of sign language. Notice in figure 23 (see below) that there are five letters in

Figure 23. The four series of the twenty original Ogham letters. The letters are read from the bottom up and then left to right. *Image shared by Runologe, CC BY-SA 4.0/Wikimedia Commons.*

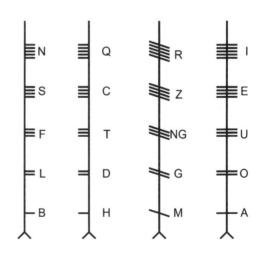

---

*This list was adapted from the list of winds in the Early Christian text *Saltair na Rann,* Canto 1, quatrains 12 to 24, as well as by Jean Wright Popescul's *The Twelve Winds of the Ancient Gaelic World* (no longer in print).

each set, with up to five lines moving in one of four directions of the alphabet: right, left, slanted, and across. Five is the number of fingers on the human hand and we know that Druids used sign language on their nose (Nose Ogham), shin (Shin Ogham), and palm (Palm Ogham).

Shin Ogham was done this way: "The fingers of the hand about the shinbone for the letters and to put them on the right of the shinbone for group B. To the left for group H. Athwart the shinbone for group M. Straight across for group A, viz, one finger for the first letter of the group, two for the second letter, till it would reach five for the fifth letter of whichever group it be."

Nose Ogham was done like this: "The fingers of the hands about the nose viz, similiter (in like manner) to right and left, athwart, across."[4] There aren't many descriptions of Palm Ogham, maybe because it was too obvious.

When inscribed, the letters would have been carved onto the side of a stone or on wood. In fact, the word *Ogham* may come from the Celtic *ogmios*, perhaps from PIE *hog-mo-* "trajectory, furrow, track," as in to plow a line into something.[5] The letters were read from the bottom up when inscribed on a stone. The letters were also written horizontally on vellum manuscripts and read across the page from left to right.

You can make your own set of Ogham divination cards on paper or burn or paint the letters onto small stones or sticks.

The Trees of the Ogham Alphabet

Each of the letters in the Ogham alphabet is represented by a plant. The original twenty "trees" of the Ogham (some of them are vines, flowers, and bushes) define a mature forest. On land where all these are found, there will be food, medicine, shelter, and fuel for all, at least in the Irish landscape.

THE OGHAM ALPHABET AND CORRESPONDING TREES

Tree	Letter	Letter Name	Pronunciation
Birch	B	Beith	BAYH
Rowan (Mountain Ash)	L	Luis	LOOS
Alder	F	Fearn	Fee-AHRN
Willow	S	Saille	SAHL-yeh
Ash	N	Nuin/Nin	NEWIN/NIN
Hawthorn	H	Huathe	HOO-uh
Oak	D	Dair	DAhoir-eh
Holly	T	Tinne	TING-yuh
Hazel	C	Coll	KUHL
Apple	Q	Quert/Cert	OOERT/KERT
Vine	M	Muin	MWIN
Ivy	G	Gort	GohRd
Reed	NG	Ngetal	NYAY-tuhl
Blackthorn	Z	Straif	SRAYF
Elder	R	Ruis	ROO-ees
Silver Fir	A	Ailm	AE-LUHM
Furze (Gorse)	O	Ohn	ON
Heather	U	Ur	OOR
Poplar (Aspen)	E	Edad/Eadha	EH-duth/EAH
Yew	I	Idad	ID-DUTH

Here is just a cursory glance at some of the meanings attached symbolically to each Ogham tree:

 Birch

A tree of new beginnings because birch is one of the first trees to colonize a disturbed area. A tree of Goddess energy, of organizing your life, and of cleaning up your act. Birch is a traditional wood for brooms (they were once made with Ash handles, Birch bristles, and Willow bindings), and the tea of the twigs can be used to cut grease and clean the stove. The Birch polypore mushroom grows exclusively on Birches and is both antiviral and antibacterial. Birch sap has antitumor qualities.

 ## Rowan (Mountain Ash)

A protective tree—invoke it to strengthen your magical shields. The ripe berries are simmered with apples and honey to make a remedy for chest colds and fevers. Wear a necklace of the berries to protect yourself from ill-intentioned magic. European Mountain Ash (Rowan) has red berries. American Mountain Ash has orange berries. The medicinal and magical properties are the same.

 ## Alder

A tree that likes to grow near water yet never rots. It was once used to craft lake dwellings and structures in or close to water. Use it to build a bridge over an uncomfortable situation and to rise above passions and conflict. The astringent inner bark makes a wound wash that pulls the edges of a lesion together.

 ## Willow

A tree that bends easily and whispers softly. Sacred to poets, it grows near water and is influenced by the Moon. The tree used to make harps. The inner bark is soothing to pain, fevers, and inflammations.

 ## Ash

A strong tree that spans the three worlds. Sacred to rulers, it was used to make thrones, shields, spears, and bows. A tree of mastery and courage, it courts the flash of lightning, a sign of the God's attention, and survives. Ash makes a very hot firewood. The young leaves are cathartic and cleansing in the very early spring.

 ## Hawthorn

A Fairy tree; sleep under a blooming "Thorn" to see the Fairies. Sacred to Beltaine, it has lovely spring blossoms but beware the thorns. A tree of poetic satire composed by the Bards. The young leaves, flowers and berries are a tonic for the heart.

 ## Oak

A tree of solidity, truth, and steadfastness. Oak spans the Three Worlds, and its roots delve as deep as the tree is high. It attracts lightning, the attention of the Goddesses and Gods, and survives. Oak is a doorway to the Celtic mysteries. Sacred to the High Goddesses and Gods, its wood is appropriate for all ritual fires. The inner bark and young leaves (picked before Summer Solstice) make a wound wash. The inner bark of White Oak can be taken as a tea for chest congestion all year.

 ## Holly

The tree that makes the hottest fire and was once used to make charcoal. A warrior tree with leaves that prick and blood-red berries. The leaves of English Holly make a tea for coughs, colds, and flu.

 ## Hazel

The tree of scholars and of learning, sacred to the Salmon of Wisdom. Hazel helps you get back to Source. Hazel twigs are the preferred wood for water dowsing. Eating hazelnuts can benefit the kidneys. In ancient times hazelnuts were added to oatmeal as a strengthening food for invalids.

Apple

A tree of love magic that shelters and feeds many lives. The Ogham letter *Quert* probably comes from *Ceirt*, an Old Irish term for Apple tree or "a bush." In British lore the word *Avalon* may be derived from the Welsh *Ynys Afallon* or *Ynys Afallach*: the Isle of Apples. Cut an apple in half and find a pentagram. Apples eaten whole and baked with the skin on are laxative, eaten peeled and raw they are antidiarrheal.

 Vine

A "tree" of struggle and of sacrificing your life's blood. The idea of grapes and wine could be a later, Christian interpretation, because grapes are not native to Ireland. *Muin* is possibly from the old kennings that give "neck" or "yolk," implying either hard work or slaughter, as when an animal's neck is cut.[6] Grape juice and grapes benefit the heart, circulation, and blood pressure and help to clean the liver.

 Ivy

The word for the Ogham alphabet letter representing Ivy, *gort*, actually means "garden." The flowers are an important last food for bees in late fall, and the leaves are fodder for cows when the grasses fail. The berries feed the birds in winter. The leaves are used to poultice ulcers, swellings, abscesses, and boils.

 Reed

The "robe" of physicians who once used the hollow stems to blow medicine onto a patient's throat. Reed is a straight guide to what and who needs healing. The roots lower fever, stop cough, clean the blood and liver, increase urination, and remove stones.

Blackthorn

A tree of strife and ill omen. A tree of winter and of battle. *Shillelaghs* (clubs) are made from its wood. The berries are used to flavor Sloe Gin. The juice of the berries can soothe a sore throat; the root bark will help a fever.

 ## Elder

A tree sacred to a Spirit called the Elder Mother and beloved of the Fairies. Never cut one down as that brings bad luck. The flower tea heals a child's fever. The berries build blood and repel a virus.

 ## Silver Fir

The tallest of trees in Europe, it bestows "eagle vision" and gives a new, larger perspective on things. The buds prevent infection, the leaves are expectorant and soothing to the lungs.

 ## Furze (Gorse)

A tree that feeds the horses; when the prickly bushes are burned to the ground, the new shoots nourish the finest steeds. The letter "O" (from *Onn*) depicts a wheel, which helps the horse accomplish its work. Use it to move forward in life. The flower tea helps jaundice and scarlet fever.

 ## Heather

This herb grows close to the cold ground, the place we all return to in the end. The flowers make a shroud for the dead. The branches are used to stuff a mattress, which brings a deep, restful sleep. The flowering tops make a wound wash. The tea of the flowers cleans the liver and blood, is sedative, and benefits fevers.

Poplar (Aspen)

Trembling Aspen Poplar leaves carry our messages to the Goddesses and Gods and to the Spirits of the dead. Send a message to the wind via the leaves. The resinous winter buds are used in healing salves, in teas for colds and sore throats, and as a wash for burns and inflammations.

 ### Yew

A tree of life, death, and rebirth, capable of living forever if allowed. The mother tree sends up a ring of daughter trees from her roots, before she dies back. A poisonous tree, only the red flesh of the berry is edible, yet the green shoots and bark have given us a cure for breast and ovarian cancers.

The idea of using these trees for divination is somewhat speculative, but there is evidence in the stories that Ogham was once used for spells. Ogma, the creator of Ogham, and Cú Chulainn carved the letters onto sticks to communicate and for magical reasons. The divinatory system does work—you can simply ask a question and pull one card (or stone, wooden stick, or other item) or lay out three cards for past, present, and future. Other spreads such as the Celtic Cross, commonly used in Tarot readings, will provide finer detail.

The best way to learn the trees is to find a live tree from the alphabet growing in nature and sit with it for several seasons. Let the tree speak to you and reveal its meaning, and then devise your own system of correspondences. Using a three cauldrons meditation for this will give very good results (see page 127).

There are many other Oghams. A trained Druid poet or Bard was expected to learn about one hundred and fifty of them. There was Bird Ogham, River Ogham, Cow Ogham, and many more. There was even musical note Ogham—messages could be sent by simply plucking notes on a harp to communicate secretly with other Druids. But the Tree Ogham is still a very good place to start! The meaning of each tree in the alphabet is profound and worthy of deeper study. As a Druid you should also experiment with creating your own Ogham alphabet.

You can read much more about the traditional spiritual, medicinal, and practical uses of these trees in my book *A Druid's Herbal of Sacred Tree Medicine* (Destiny Books, 2008).

Ogham

*Beith—First comes the letter **B***
*That is for the **Birch**, you see*
*Luis—The next one that comes is the letter **L***
*The **Rowan** tree that's good for a spell*
*Fearn—Then comes F—the **Alder** letter*
*Saille—and S for **Willow**—both like things wetter*
*Nuin—**Ash** is N—a wise old tree*
*Huath—and H is for **Hawthorn**—the gate to Fairy*
*Dair—Next, **D** is for **Oak** that courts the flash*
*Tinne—While **T** is for **Holly** that burns fire to ash*
*Coll—C is for **Hazel**, whose nuts are for cracking*
*Quert—and **Q** is for **Apple**—on which deer are snacking*
*Muin—M is a mystery—bleeding red **Grape** or **Bramble***
*Gort—G is **Ivy**—a fodder for the humble*
*Pethbok/Ngetal—P/NG is **Reed**, so useful for healing*
*Straif—Another S is **Blackthorn**—makes wounds with no sealing*
*Ruis—R gives us **Elder**—the Fairy Mother*
*Ailm—While A above **Silver Fir** does hover*
*Ohn—O is for **Gorse**—and a wheel pulled by horses*
*Uhr—U is for **Heather**, and coldest, dark sources*
*Eadha—E gives us **Poplar**—whispering messages of worth*
*Idad—I is for **Yew**—tree of death and rebirth*

Ellen Evert Hopman

Charms for Abundance, Healing, and Protection

Three things without which the protection of the Gods cannot be: forgiving an enemy and a wrong done, wisdom in judgement and act, and cleaving to what is just, come what may.

ANCIENT IRISH TRIAD

As a Druid you should be at least somewhat familiar with the old charms and incantations. Here is a smattering of what can be found in the literature. White Oak Druids and Tribe of the Oak Druids study these charms to empower their own magic.

Charm for Abundance

The poem below is adapted from the *Carmina Gadelica*. I have substituted Brighid, the "Mary of the Gael," for the Christian Mary. She can be thought of as the Saint or the Goddess.

The charm sent of [Brighid],
To the [woman] who was dwelling
On the floor of the glen,
On the cold high moors—
 On the floor of the glen,
 On the cold high moors.

She put spell to saliva,
To increase her butter,
To decrease her milk,
To make plentiful her food—
> *To increase her butter,*
> *To decrease her milk,*
> *To make plentiful her food.*[1]

Healing Charms

The indigestion charm is intended for livestock that chew cud, but it can easily be adapted for people with stomach issues, the flu, and other conditions. The original invokes Columba—the man who converted the Picts and Scots to Christianity—but I have adapted it by substituting the herbalists' Goddess Airmid.

The spell made by [Airmid],
To the one cow of the woman,
For the [sore mouth], for the gum disease,
For the bag, for the swelling,
For the indigestion;

For the flux disease,
For the cud disease,
For the [stomach] disease,
For the [digestion] disease,
For the surfeit;

For the [painful] disease,
For the [cramping] disease,
For the water disease,
For the red disease,
For the madness;

I will cleave the [sore mouth],
I will cleave the gum disease,
I will cleave the bag,
I will cleave the [swelling],
And I will kill the indigestion;

I will cleave the flux,
I will cleave the cud,
I will cleave the [stomach],
I will cleave the [digestion],
And drive away the surfeit;

I will cleave the [pain],
I will cleave the [cramping],
I will cleave the water,
I will cleave the red,
And wither will the madness.[2]

Healing for a Child

A healing charm from *Carmina Gadelica* written in the form of a lullaby to be sung to an ailing child. It is based on a tale where a woman nurses an ailing swan back to health and finds her sick child's health restored at the same time. The original is a petition to Mary, but here also, I have substituted Brighid. The original song also has the refrain "Hu hi! Ho ho!" in between each line.

Lullaby

Oh, white swan,
Sad your condition,
Pitiful your state,
Your blood is flowing,
Oh, white swan,

Far from your friends,
Dame of thy converse,
Remain near me,
Healer of gladness you,
Bless my little child,
Shield him from death,
Hasten him to health,
As you desire,
Pain and sorrow
To your injurer,
A thousand welcomes to you,
Life and health be yours,
The age of joy be yours,
In every place,
Peace and growth to him,
Strength and worth to him,
Victory of place,
Everywhere to him,
Blessed [Brighid],
Fair white lovely,
Cuddling you,
Hugging you,
Bathing you,
Be with you,
Shielding you
From the net of your enemy;
Caressing you,
Guarding you,
Fulfilling you
The love of your mother, you,
The love of her love, you,
The love of the Spirits, you,
And the Gods of life![3]

Charm for Protection

This charm is a prayer for long life addressed to the pagan divinities for a long life, good fortune, and lasting fame translated in Kuno Meyer's *Miscellanea Hibernica*. It is ascribed to Fer fio and in it, life is regarded as a journey into the Plain of Age.

Prayer for Long Life

I invoke the seven daughters of the sea,
who fashion the threads of the sons of long life.
> *May three deaths be taken from me!*
> *May three periods of age be granted to me!*
> *May seven waves of good fortune be dealt to me!*
Phantoms shall not harm me on my journey
in flashing corslet without hindrance.
My fame shall not perish.
May old age come to me! Death shall not come to me till
> *I am old.*
I invoke my Silver Champion who has not died, who will
> *not die.*
May a time be granted to me of the quality of white
> *bronze!*
> *May my double be slain!*
> *May my right be maintained!*
> *May my strength be increased!*
> *Let my grave not be ready!*
Death shall not come to me on an expedition.
May my journey be carried to the end!
The headless adder shall not seize me,
nor the hard-gray worm,
nor the headless black chafer.
Neither thief shall harm me,
nor a band of women, nor a band of armed men.

Let increase of time come to me from the King of the
    Universe!
I invoke Senach of the seven periods of time,
whom fairy women have reared on the breasts of plenty
    May my seven candles not be extinguished!
      I am an indestructible stronghold,
      I am an unshaken rock,
      I am a precious stone,
      I am the luck of the week.
May I live a hundred times a hundred years,
each hundred of them apart!
I summon their boons to me . . . [4]

The number seven is repeated extensively in this charm. It may be a reference to the seven planets that were known at that time.

Smooring the Fire to Protect the Home

Smooring the fire each night was an important job for women in Celtic areas, as was uncovering the fire in the morning. In ancient times ashes would have been piled over the smoldering peat to keep the embers alive through the night.

The hearth was a type of fire altar where herbs or offerings of food were given to the flames, to protect the house by warding off storms and bad Spirits. The hearth fire was also a sacred method of purification for New Year's rituals as in Scotland at Hogmanay (New Years) when Juniper was burned and the whole house smudged by the smoke. Juniper could also be used as a smudge in the house and barn any time purification was needed.*

---

*Juniper was an herb favored in all northern European cultures, for purification by smoke.

How to Smoor the Fire

To do this, the embers are evenly spread and formed into a circle. The circle is then divided into three equal sections, and a peat is laid between each section, each peat touching center. As each peat is laid down, a deity or power is invoked. The circle is then covered over with ashes sufficient to preserve it through the night. When the smooring is complete the woman closes her eyes, stretches out her hand, and softly intones a prayer.

Druids can invoke the Three Worlds (Ancestors, Nature Spirits, and Goddesses and Gods, or Land, Sea, and Sky) or any three deities or triple deity they might be working with. Below is an invocation for smooring the fire from *Carmina Gadilica*.

The sacred Three
To save,
To shield,
To surround
The hearth,
The house,
The household,
This eve,
This night,
Oh! This eve,
This night,
And every night,
Each single night.[5]

Herbal Charms and Spells

Three candles that illumine every darkness: truth, nature, and knowledge.

Ancient Irish Triad

For the Druids, herbalism was a magical art as well as a medical one, and there are ancient magical incantations and spells that will aid you in your Druidic healing practice. Take the time to learn at least some herbalism and basic first aid. Just as Vedic physicians once sang over their plants and patients, the Druids very likely did the same.

Medicinal Herbalism

The *Rig Veda* is the oldest Vedic-Sanskrit sacred text, it may have been composed as early as 1900 BCE, in India. It is a collection of hymns of praise and sacred knowledge. The following is an excerpt from a hymn in the *Rig Veda* that a physician would have chanted as she gathered and prepared herbs or administered them to a patient.

The Healing Plants

*Mothers, you have a hundred forms and a thousand
    growths. You who have a hundred ways of working,
    make this man whole for me.*

*Be joyful, you plants that bear the flowers and those that
    bear fruit. Like mares that win the race together, the
    growing plants will carry us across.*

You mothers who are called plants, I say to you who are
goddesses: let me win a horse, a cow, and robe—and
your very life, O man . . .
Like cows from the cow-pen, out stream the powers of the
plants that will win wealth—and your life, O man . . .
When I take these plants in my hand, yearning for the
victory prize, the life of the disease vanishes . . .
Fly away, disease, along with the blue jay and the jay;
disappear with the howl of the wind, with the rain
storm . . .
Do not harm the man who digs you up, nor him for whom
I dig you up; let all our two-footed and four-footed
creatures be without sickness.
You growing plants who hear this, and those who have gone
far away, all coming together unite your power in this
plant . . .
Plant, you are supreme; the trees are your subjects . . . [1]

While the Celtic Druids did not write these kinds of things down
(they were kept in the oral tradition), we are fortunate to have a wonderful collection of traditional hymns and incantations collected in the
Hebrides of Scotland at the turn of the past century. This is a small
selection of a few of them from *Carmina Gadelica* that you can incorporate into your Druidic healing practice.

When picking Yarrow:

The Yarrow

I will pluck the yarrow fair,
That more benign shall be my face,
That more warm shall be my lips,
That more chaste shall be my speech,
Be my speech the beams of the sun,
Be my lips the sap of the strawberry.

May I be an isle in the sea,
May I be a hill on the shore,
May I be a star in waning of the moon,
May I be a staff to the weak,
Wound can I every man,
Wound can no man me.[2]

When picking Saint John's Wort:

Saint John's Wort

Saint John's wort, Saint John's wort,
My envy whosoever has thee,
I will pluck thee with my right hand,
I will preserve thee with my left hand,
Whoso findeth thee in the cattle fold,
Shall never be without kine.[3]

When plucking the Shamrock:

The Shamrock of Power

Thou shamrock of foliage,
Thou shamrock of power,
Thou shamrock of foliage,
Which [the Goddess] had under the bank,*
Thou shamrock of my love,
Of most beauteous hue,
I would choose thee in death,
To grow on my grave,
    I would choose thee in death,
    To grow on my grave.[4]

---

*The original names Mary.

The Apple Tree

O apple tree
Apple branch
Apple tree
Tree of apples . . .

O apple tree, may the Gods be with thee,
May the moon and the sun be with thee,
May the east and west winds be with thee,
May everything that ever existed be with thee,
May every bounty and desire be with thee,
May every passion and divinity be with thee,
May great Somerled* and his band be with thee,
May everyone, like myself, be with thee.[5]

Herbal Magic

Three signs of cruelty: Needlessly to frighten an animal,
needlessly tearing trees and plants, and to be insistent in
asking favors

ANCIENT IRISH TRIAD

Numerous books will point you to specific herbs and trees to use for magic, but the very best way to learn these practices is to find a few native herbs that grow in your area and employ them in your own original plant spells. The more passion and emotion you can channel into the project, the more effective the working will be. But please remember that all energy you send out comes back to you three times, and it's always best to design a working that will affect the highest good for all concerned.

If you memorize these few basic principles of herb magic you can use just about any plant to craft an appropriate spell:

---

*A famous warrior (d.1164) who defended Scotland from the Norse

Roots: Roots will help you ground. Wear them and drink or eat them to contact the Underworld of the Sidhe (Fairies), the Beloved Dead, Underworld deities, the Ancestors, and to understand hidden forces and dark secrets.

Bark: The outer bark of trees and shrubs is protective to them and to you. Wear a piece of the bark or drink a bark tea to strengthen your personal protection and magical shields.

Leaves: Leaves are manifestations of a plant's energy and growth. Drink leaf teas, eat edible leaves and wear leaves to increase your strength, health, enthusiasm, and will to keep going.

Highly aromatic plants: Aromatic herbs and resins have disinfectant properties. Use these plants for healing, purification, and consecration. Make a tea with these fragrant herbs and spray or asperge it around the ritual area. Make a wash for the floor, burn them as incense, add them to a purifying bath or wear them as perfume, oils, or in a sachet.

Flowers: Flowers are the sex organs of plants. Their fragrance and beauty will increase your personal magnetism, attractiveness, fertility, and sexual pleasure. Drink a flower tea, wear the buds in a sachet, or add flowers to your bath to lighten your spirit and to attract love.

Fruits: Fruits are the final manifestation of a plant's life work. They are all about wealth, abundance, and success. Leave out bowls of fruit to attract prosperity. Eat fruits to both cleanse and build your body.

Nuts and seeds: Every seed has inside it the potential for a new beginning. Seeds carry the possibilities of transition, change, renewal of cycles, and the future. Seeds such as Walnuts ease mental struggles and nourish the brain. Masses of small seeds, like Mustard Seeds, can be used in workings to multiply or grow something.

Vines: Vines that cling, like Ivy, are used to bind the objects of a spell. Use them to pull things together.

Stinging herbs and thorns: These can be used to repel evil; make a thorny wreath or hang bunches of stinging plants like Nettles on gateposts and doors to keep noxious forces at bay.

A Small Selection of Herb Spells from the Scottish Celtic Tradition

> . . . *an old man in Uist said that he used to swim to an islet in a lake in his neighborhood for ivy, woodbine, and mountain ash. These, sometimes separately and sometimes combined, he twined into a three-plied "cuach," ring, which he placed over the lintel of his cow-house and under the vessels in his milk-house, to safeguard his cows and his milk from witchcraft, evil eye, and murrain.*
>
> CARMINA GADELICA, VOLUME II, 1900, 280.

 Elder

Latin name: *Sambucus* spp.
Irish: Trom
Ogham letter name: Ruis

Medicinally Elder is safe for both children and adults. In the case of fever, flu, or another virus take Elderberry tea or tincture every two hours in hot water. For magical purposes apply the fresh juice of the inner bark to your eyelids to acquire the second sight. Sleep under an Elder at Samhuinn or at Bealltan (Scottish spellings) to see the Fairies. But remember to always be respectful of the plant and never cut an Elder down as it's bad luck and it angers the Fairies.

Below are a few suggestions for integrating the protective magic of Elder into your practices.

- Make an equal armed solar cross from the twigs bound with red thread and hang it over the door, place it in a window, or hang it in the barn. It will repel evil.
- Make a very small equal-armed Elder twig cross bound with red thread and wear it on your person.
- Place dried Elder berries on your windowsill to prevent evil from entering.
- Carry Elder wood to guard against ghosts—hearse drivers once used Elder whips for this reason.
- Plant an Elder near the house to stop ghosts and psychic attacks.
- Make a wreath of Elder and Wormwood and hang it on the door or on a gatepost to repel evil.
- Wrap Elder and Wormwood around the milk churn to keep Fairies and sorcerers from spoiling the milk or stealing the butter.

Ivy

Latin name: *Hedera* spp.
Irish: Eidhneán
Ogham letter name: Gort

Ivy also has many protective properties.

- Make a wreath of Ivy and Woodbine, Bramble, or Rowan (or all four) to protect the house from sorcery, from the evil eye, and to ward off cattle disease.
- Place a wreath of Dandelion and Marigold bound with a triple Ivy cord under the milk pail to prevent the milk from being charmed away by Witches or Fairies.
- If a bird steals a human's hair for its nest it can lead to headaches or baldness to the hair's owner. Counter this by wearing an Ivy crown.
- Plant or maintain Ivy growing on or near the house to protect the home from sorcery.

 **Juniper**

Latin name: *Juniperus* spp.
Irish: Aiteal
Not a part of the Ogham alphabet

Medicinally the tea of Juniper berries can be used to ease chest congestion, urinary infection, and edema. (**Caution:** do not use the berries if pregnant or if you have a kidney disease.) Juniper can be used to enhance magical work—pull the plant up by the roots with the branches separated into four separate bundles taken between five fingers while chanting a prayer.

Here are a couple ways to benefit from the protective and health-enhancing powers of Juniper:

- Burn Juniper in the hearth to repel evil Spirits and to ensure good health—especially at New Year's.
- Use Juniper as a smudge to fumigate any area (the house, the barn, tool shed, or animal enclosure) where sickness or bad luck are lingering.

 Oak

Latin name: *Quercus* spp.
Irish: Duir
Ogham letter name: Dair

Medicinally, a wash made with young Oak leaves (they must be gathered before Summer Solstice) or with the inner bark of Oak (gathered all year round) will pull the edges of a wound together. White Oak tea (*Quercus alba*), made from young leaves and/or inner bark, helps with diarrhea, sore throats, bleeding gums, and chest congestion and is used to make a compress for piles. The acorns of an Oak can be dried and made into powder to dust on old ulcers and infected wounds.

There is a traditional saying to "swear an oath by Oak and Ash, and

Thorn" (*Thorn* is Hawthorn) as these three trees are favorites of the Fairies and where they grow together, one is very likely to see Fairies.

Some ways to receive the empowering and protective magic of the mighty Oak:

- Carry acorns in your pockets for fertility.
- Place a piece of lightning-struck Oak in a charm bag to empower any working or spell.
- Make an equal-armed solar cross with Oak twigs and bind it with red thread. Hang it in the home for protection.
- Make a small equal-armed solar cross with Oak to wear around your neck or hide in your clothing.

 ## Rowan, Mountain Ash, Wizard's Tree, or Druid's Tree

Latin name: *Sorbus* spp.
Irish: Caorthann
Ogham letter name: Luis

A Highland medicinal cure for coughs, colds, and sore throats is to simmer the ripe Rowan berries with apple slices and honey to make a syrup. Rowan berries have more vitamin C than lemons!

For magic, the time to gather Rowan wood is on Beltaine Eve. Rowan is the food of the Fairies—the original Rowan berries came to this world from the Land of the Sidhe. Use your gathered Rowan wood to build a ritual fire or wood knife to use as your *athame* (ritual blade)—do not use an iron knife or blade as that repels the Fairies.

To enhance the protective magic of Rowan for yourself and your animal friends:

- In the fall gather the red berries (or orange berries of the American Mountain Ash, which have the same properties) and thread them on red thread to be worn as a protective necklace.
- Make a wreath of the branches or an equal-armed solar cross of

the twigs bound with red thread and hang it to protect the house.

- ᷓ Make a tiny equal armed cross from the twigs bound with red thread and hide it in your clothing as protection.
- ᷓ When mating your cow to a bull, make a wreath of Rowan and Ivy, pass it over a sacred fire three times, and put it on the cow the night before.
- ᷓ Make a large wreath and pass a sick animal through it. Or place a wreath around your dog, cat, horse, or cow's neck as a protective charm. You can also tie Rowan to your horse's tail.
- ᷓ Tie bunches of Rowan and Honeysuckle or Woodbine together and hang them in the barn to protect the cattle.

Willow

Latin plant name: *Salix* spp.
Irish: Saileach
Ogham letter name: Saille

Medicinally Willow bark tea relives aches, pains, and inflammations.

Magically Willow is a tree sacred to poets and harps are made from its wood. Sit under a Willow to incubate a poem. Willow can also promote fertility by placing a branch of Willow under the bed.

Woodbine, Honeysuckle

Latin plant name: *Lonicera periclymenum*
Irish: Féithleann
Not a part of the Ogham alphabet

Hoops of Woodbine combined with the energy of the moon create powerful magic:

- ᷓ Cut Woodbine under the March full Moon and make a wreath of it. Smoke the wreath over the ritual fire and then hang it to attract joy.

🌤 Cut Woodbine at the waxing Moon, smoke it over the ritual fire, and make a hoop to pass a sick child through or pass a large hoop over a sick adult three times.

The Secret Names of Plants

Double, double toil and trouble;
Fire burn and cauldron bubble.
Fillet of a fenny snake,
in the cauldron boil and bake;
Eye of newt and toe of frog,
Wool of bat and tongue of dog,
Adder's fork and blind-worm's sting,
Lizard's leg and Howlet's wing,
For a charm of powerful trouble,
Like a Hell-broth boil and bubble . . .

MACBETH: ACT FOUR, SCENE 1,
BY WILLIAM SHAKESPEARE

Here is a bit of British magical herb lore from the Shakespearian era when Hedge Druids, Cunning Men, Wise Women, midwives, and herbalists were being persecuted as "Witches." Of necessity they used nicknames for plants, probably as self-defense in case they got caught with a grimoire (a book of magical spells, incantations, and recipes) and also to keep the lore secret from non-practitioners.

The table on pages 185 to 190 is a collection of several such secret names, including those used by Shakespeare in the famous quote above. Use these terms as you craft your own magical potions. They will also help you to understand recipes in old grimoires.

SECRET PLANT NAMES*

Secret Name	Common Herb Name	Latin Name
Adder's Fork	Bisort	*Polygonum bistorta*
Adder's Mouth	Chickweed	*Stellaria media*
Bat's Wings	Holly	*Ilex* spp.
Blind Worm's Sting	Knotweed	*Polygonum* spp.
Blood	Elder tree sap or the sap of another tree	
Blood of Kronos	sap of Cedar	*Cedrus* spp.
Blood of Hephaistos	Wormwood	*Artemisia absinthium*
Blood of Hestia	Chamomile	*Matricaria recutita, Anthemis nobilis*
Blood of a Titan	Wild Lettuce	*Lactuca virosa*
Bloodroot	Tormentil or Septfoil	*Sanguinaria canadensis* or *Potentilla erecta*
Bloodwort	Yarrow	*Achillea millefolium*
Brains	the congealed gum of a Cherry tree	
Bread and Cheese Tree	Hawthorn/Whitethorn or Hazel	*Crataegus* spp. or *Corylus* spp.
Broom	Gorse	*Ulex* spp.
Bull's Blood or Seed of Horus	Horehound	*Marrubium vulgare*
Buttons	Tansy	*Tanacetum vulgare*
Calf's Snout	Snapdragon	*Antirrhinum* spp.
Candlemas Maiden	Snowdrop	*Galanthus* spp.

*The secret plant names in this list have been adapted from several sources. Of course these were passed verbally as with so much magical knowledge, but the written source subsequent online sources likely originated from is *A Modern Herbal in Two Volumes* by Mrs. M. Grieve (Margaret Grieve). If you are interested in more of these secret names, a few online sources are James Fair's "What Is 'Eye of Newt'?" on his Wisdom Biscuits website (2020), Miss Witch's "Witch's Secret Names For Plants And Herbs" on her WitchesLore website (March 20, 2020), and Shirley TwoFeathers's "Old Names for Herbs" in the Magikal Ingredients section of her website (2016).

Secret Name	Common Herb Name	Latin Name
Corpse Candles	Mullein	*Verbascum* spp.
Crow Foot	Wild Geranium	*Geranium maculatum*
Cuckoo's Bread	Common Plantain	*Plantago major*
Dead Man's Ash	a Mandrake root poppet	*Mandragora officinarum*
Death Angel	Agaric	*Amanita ocreata*
Devil's Apple	Datura	*Datura stramonium*
Devil's Dung	Asafetida	*Ferula assa-foetida*
Dew of the Sea	Rosemary	*Salvia uricular*
Dog's Tongue	Hound's Tongue	*Cynoglossum officinale*
Dog's Tooth	Violet	*Erythronium dens-canis*
Dove's Foot	Crane's Bill/Wild Geranium	*Geranium maculatum*
Dragon's Blood	Calamus, Sweet Flag	*Acorus calamus*
Dragon's Scales, Dragonwort	Bistort Leaves	*Bistorta officinalis*
Duck's Foot	May Apple	*Podophyllum peltatum*
Earth Smoke	Fumitory	*Fumaria officinalis*
Elf Dock	Elecampane	*Inula helenium*
Elf Leaf	Rosemary or Lavender	*Rosmarinus officinalis* or *Lavandula* spp.
Elf's Wort, Elfwort	Elecampane	*Inula helenium*
Enchanter's Plant	Vervain	*Verbena officinalis*
Eye of the Day	Common Daisy	*Bellis perennis*
Eye of Newt	Mustard Seed or Wild Mustard Seed	*Brassica* spp. or *Sinapis arvensis*
Fairy's Finger	Foxglove	*Digitalis* spp.
Fairy's Horses	Ragwort	*Jacobaea vulgaris*
Fairy Bells	Wood Sorrel or Bluebells	*Oxalis acetosella* or *Hyacinthoides non-scripta*

Secret Name	Common Herb Name	Latin Name
Fairy Cup	Cowslip	*Primula veris*
Fairy Queen	Lady's Slipper	genus *Cypripedium*
Fairy Smoke	Indian Pipe	*Monotropa uniflora*
Fenny Snake	Jack-in-the-Pulpit	*Arisaema tryphyllum*
Five Fingers	Cinquefoil	genus *Potentilla*
Graveyard Dust	Mullein	*Verbascum thapsus*
Hag's Taper	Great Mullein	*Verbascum uricul*
Hagthorn	Hawthorn	*Crataegus* spp.
Hair of Venus	Maidenhair Fern	*Adiantum* spp.
Herb of Grace	Vervain	*Verbena officinalis*
Holy Herb	Yerba Santa	*Eriodictyon sp. Benth.*
Horse Hoof	Coltsfoot	*Tussilago farfara*
Howlet's Wing	Garlic	*Allium sativum*
Joy of the Mountain	Marjoram	*Origanum majorana*
Jupiter's Staff	Great Mullein	*Verbascum thapsus*
Knight's Milfoil	Yarrow	*Achillea millefolium*
Lad's Love	Southernwood	*Artemisia abrotanum*
Lady's Glove	Foxglove aka Witches' Gloves	*Digitalis* spp.
Lady's Slipper	American Valerian	genus *Cypripedium*
Lamb's Ears	Betony	*Stachys* spp.
Lion's Ear or Tail	Motherwort	*Leonurus cardiaca*
Lion's Tooth	Dandelion, Priest's Crown	*Taraxacum* spp.
Little Dragon	Tarragon, Estragon	*Artemisia dracunculus*
Lizard's Leg	Ivy	*Hedera helix*
Love Lies Bleeding	Amaranth	*Amaranthus* spp.
Love Root	Orris root	*Uricul iridis*

Secret Name	Common Herb Name	Latin Name
Man's Health	Ginseng	*Panax ginseng*
Master of the Woods	Woodruff	*Galium odoratum*
May Rose	Black Haw	*Viburnum prunifolium*
Maypops	Passion Flower	*Passiflora incanata*
Mother's Heart	Shepherd's Purse	*Capsella bursa-pastoris*
Mouse's Ear	Hawk Weed	*Hieracium* spp.
Mouse's Tail	Common Stonecrop	*Sedum acre*
Nose Bleed	Yarrow	*Achillea millefolium*
Old-Maid's-Nightcap	Wild Geranium	*Geranium maculatum*
Old Man	Mugwort	*Artemisia vulgaris*
Old Man's Flannel	Great Mullein	*Verbascum thapsus*
Old Man's Pepper	Yarrow	*Achillea millefolium*
Old Woman	Wormwood	*Artemisia absinthium*
Paddock Pipes	Horsetail	*Equisetum* spp.
Pantagruelian	Marijuana	*Cannabis* spp.
Pig's Tail	Arnica, Leopard's Bane	*Arnica montana*
Queen of the Meadow	Meadowsweet	*Filipendula ulmaria*
Queen of the Meadow Root, Sweet Joe Pye Root	Gravelroot	*Eupatorium purpureum*
Queen of the Night	Vanilla Cactus, Night Blooming Cereus	*Selenicereus uricularas*
Queen's Root	Stillingia, Silverleaf	*Stillingia sylvatica*
Red Cockscomb	Amaranth	*Amaranthus caudatus*
Ring-o-Bells	Bluebells	*Hyacinthoides non-scripta*
Robin-Run-in-the-Grass	Goosegrass	*Eleusine indica*
Scaldhead	Blackberry	*Rubus fructicosus*
Semen of Ares	Clover	*Medicago sativa*
Semen of Helios	White Hellebore	*Veratrum album*

Secret Name	Common Herb Name	Latin Name
Semen of Hermes	Dill	*Anethum graveolens*
Semen of Hephaistos	Fleabane	*Erigeron annuus, Erigeron strigosus*
Seed of Horus	White Horehound	*Marrubium vulgare*
Silver Branch	Apple	*Pyrus malus, Malus* spp.
Skull	Skullcap Mushroom, Autumn Skullcap, Deadly Galerina	*Galerina marginata*
Son-Before-the-Father, *Filium ante Pater*	Coltsfoot	*Tussilago farfara*
Sorcerer's Berry	Belladonna	*Atropa belladonna*
Sorcerer's Root	Mandrake	*Atropa mandragora*
Sorcerer's Violet	Periwinkle	*Vinca minor*
Star Flower	Borage	*Borago officinalis*
Starweed	Chickweed	*Stellaria media*
Tanner's Bark	Common Oak	*Quercus* spp.
Thor's Helper	Rowan	*Sorbus* spp.
Toe of Frog	Bulbous Buttercup leaves	*Ranunculus acris*
Tongue of Dog	Hound's Tongue	*Cynoglossum officinale*
Torches	Great Mullein	*Verbascum thapsus*
Tree of Enchantment	White Willow	*Salix alba*
Tree of Life	White Cedar	*Thuja occidentalis*
Tree of Love	Apple	*Pyrus malus, Malus* spp.
Unicorn's Horn	True Unicorn Root or False Unicorn	*Aletris farinosa* or *Helonias dioica*
Unicorn Root	Boneset or Ague Root, Star Grass	*Eupatorium perfoliatum* or *Aletris uricula*
Unshoe-the-Horse	Moonwort Fern	*Botrychium lunaria*
Water Dragon	Marsh Marigold	*Caltha palustris*
Witch Bells	Foxglove	*Digitalis* spp.

Secret Name	Common Herb Name	Latin Name
Witch Herb	Mugwort	*Artemisia vulgaris*
Witch Tree or Wood	Mountain Ash, Rowan	*Sorbus* spp.
Witchen	Rowan	*Sorbus aucuparia*
Witch's Aspirin	White Willow, Willow bark	*Salix alba*
Witch's Brier	Dog Rose	*Rosa canina*
Witch's Gloves	Foxglove	*Digitalis* spp.
Witch's Hair	Dodder	*Cuscuta* spp.
Witch's Herb	Sweet Basil	*Ocimum basilicum*
Witch's Thimble	Datura	*Datura stramonium*
Witch's Weed	Cinquefoil	*Potentilla reptans*, *Potentilla erecta*
Witchbane	Rowan	*Sorbus americana*, *Sorbus aucuparia*
Wolf Claw	Club Moss	*Lycopodium clavatum*
Wolf's Hat	Wolfsbane	*Aconitum* spp.
Wood Ear	a Fungus on Elder or Elm	*Auricularia uricular-judae*
Wool of Bat	Moss	*Bryophyta* spp.
Worms	the thin gnarled roots of a tree	

How to Tell Time by the Flowers

As an astute Druid you don't need to be tied to a cell phone or wrist-watch. You should know by the Sun's position what time of day it is, and by the position of the Moon and constellations what the time of night might be. You can also learn to keep time by the opening and closing of flowers. A sampling of the hours at which certain flowers open or close is shown in the table on page 191.

TELLING TIME BY FLOWERS*

Hour	Flower	Flower Behavior
2 a.m.	Common Morning Glory	opens
	Night-Blooming Cereus	closes
5 a.m.	Buttercups, Poppy, Wild Roses	opens
7 a.m.	White Water Lily, Daylily	opens
9 a.m.	Calendula (Pot marigold), Daisy	opens
	Prickly Sow Thistle	closes
10 a.m.	Star-of Bethlehem, Sorrel, Common Sow-Thistle	opens
Noon	Goatsbeard, Blue Passion Flower, Ice Plant	opens
	Morning Glories	closes
1 p.m.	Carnation	opens
	Childing Pink	closes
2 p.m.	Afternoon Squill	opens
	Water Lily, Chicory, Poppy, Potatoes, Sandworts	closes
3 p.m.	Hawkbit Calendula, Spider Plant, Pumpkin	closes
4 p.m.	Scarlet Pimpernel, Sorrel, White Water Lily	closes
6 p.m.	Moonflower	opens
8–10 p.m.	Night Flowering Cereus, Evening Primrose	opens
9 p.m.	Flowering Tobacco	opens
	Cowslip	closes

*This table was adapted from information in "How to Tell Time from Flowers with a Floral Clock" from the Weird Facts website and "The Flower Clock" from the Garden Life section of the Gardena website.

Weather Forecasting with Flowers

In general, if plants close before their regular time, you can be sure that bad weather is on the horizon.

If Marigolds have not yet opened by 7:00 a.m., this signals that the weather will be bad for the day. If they close completely, a storm is likely on its way.[6]

In dry conditions a Pinecone's scales stand separately and stiffly apart; in damp weather the scales soften and close.

Oak and Maple leaves tend to curl in high humidity, preceding a heavy rain.

If the tiny white flowers of Common Chickweed (*Stellaria media*) are closed in the morning, this means that rain is soon to fall. (The plant usually opens 9:00 a.m. to Noon).

Purple Sandwort and Scarlet Pimpernel open in sunny weather but close tightly when rain is nigh.

If the African Marigold opens later than 8:00 a.m. or closes before 5:00 p.m., rain is coming.

Wide-open Morning Glory blooms mean fair weather but closed petals indicate that rain or bad weather will soon arrive.

The Common Daisy will close its petals or droop downward when rain is immanent.

Many other flower varieties close their petals as rain draws near and open them again after the rain or the next morning—Germander Speedwell, Hieraciums, Red Campion, Succory, Tulips, White Water Lily, Wintergreen, and Wood Sorrel.

Dew on the grass at sunrise means good weather is in the offing. But, "When grass is dry at morning light, Look for rain before the night."[7]

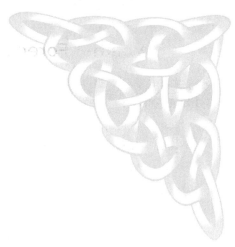

PART 3

Druids and Nature

Words of Wisdom from Fellow Druids

Revelations of Nature

By Kenneth Proefrock, NMD

Tech Duinn,* whence the name? Not hard to say. When the sons of Mil came from the west to Erin, their druid said to them, "If one of you climbs the mast," said he, "and chants incantations against the Tuatha De, before they can do so, the battle will be broken against them, and their land will be ours; and he that casts the spell will die".

THE METRICAL DINDSHENCHAS,
EDWARD GWYNN TRANSLATION

In ancient Ireland records were kept of important landscape features and events in the Dindsenchas or Dindshenchas (modern spellings: Dinnseanchas or Dinnsheanchas or Dınnṡeanċas), meaning "lore of places." It describes the origins of place names and traditions concerning events and characters that lived in or were part of important events in each locality.

As a Druid you should be well versed in the ecology and history of your own area, especially in a time of rapid global warming when it is

---

*The House of Don, the House of the Dead

*important to keep track of the changes. And on a spiritual level, you
should have an appreciation for the kinds of offerings and ceremonies
that were done on the land where you live, for millennia.*

*The Order of the White Oak and Tribe of the Oak Druid
Dr. Kenneth Proefrock contributes the following essay on the subject
(see page ix at the end of his foreword for more details about his
work).*

ELLEN EVERT HOPMAN

One of the essential principles of the Order of the White Oak's and
Tribe of the Oak's approach to spiritual engagement with the surrounding world is a deep and abiding respect for the land and the environment.
The Celtic mythologies are full of tales indicating that many aspects of
the surrounding landscape were physical incarnations of deities. Many
mountains, rivers, trees, and animals had specific deities associated with
them. The *Dindsenchas* (The Lore Concerning Places) are a series of
relatively short poems describing how and why certain places in Ireland
got their names. The Land Herself is presented as a living, breathing
persona whose permission is asked before Amergin Glúingel and the
Milesians can set foot on Her, as related in *Lebor Gabála Érenn*:

> *I invoke the land of Ireland.*
> *Much-coursed be the fertile sea,*
> *Fertile be the fruit-strewn mountain,*
> *Fruit-strewn be the showery wood,*
> *Showery be the river of water-falls,*
> *Of water-falls be the lake of deep pools,*
> *Deep pooled be the hill-top well,*
> *A well of the tribes be the assembly,*
> *An assembly of the kings be Tara,*

Tara be the hill of the tribes,
The tribes of the sons of Mil,
Of Mil be the ships the barks,
Let the lofty bark be Ireland,
Lofty Ireland Darkly sung,
An incantation of great cunning;
The great cunning of the wives of Bres,
The wives of Bres of Buaigne;
The great lady Ireland,
Eremon hath conquered her,
Ir, Eber have invoked for her.
I invoke the land of Ireland.

LEBOR GABÁLA ÉRENN,
ORIGINAL TEXT EDITED AND TRANSLATED
BY R. A. STEWART MACALISTER

Amergin Glúingel, the poet-Druid of the Milesians was one of the most powerful Irish Filidh. It is clear that he believed that the Land was a living, potent entity that had a name and, therefore, deserved respect. Amergin as he sets his right foot on the land of Éire, recites this famous song:

I am a wind on the sea
I am a wave of the ocean
I am the roar of the sea,
I am a powerful ox,
I am a hawk on a cliff,
I am a dewdrop in the sunshine,
I am a boar for valor,
I am a salmon in pools,
I am a lake in a plain,
I am the strength of art,
I am a spear with spoils that wages battle,

I am a man that shapes fire for a head.
Who clears the stone-place of the mountain?
What the place in which the setting of the sun lies?
Who has sought peace without fear seven times?
Who names the waterfalls?
Who brings his cattle from the house of Tethra?
What person, what god Forms weapons in a fort?
In a fort that nourishes satirists,
Chants a petition, divides the Ogam letters,
Separates a fleet, has sung praises?
A wise satirist.

He sang afterward to increase fish in the creeks:

Fishful sea—
Fertile land—
Burst of fish—
Fish under wave—
With courses of birds—
Rough Sea—
A white wall—
With hundreds of salmon—
Broad Whale—
A port song—
A burst of fish.

LEBOR GABÁLA ÉRENN,
ORIGINAL TEXT EDITED AND TRANSLATED
BY R. A. STEWART MACALISTER

Our Celtic ancestors certainly seemed to recognize the importance of the concepts of harmony and balance in nature as essential to the well-being of both the Land and its inhabitants. Amergin Glúingel seems to imply that he and his people would thrive in the new Land provided they respected Her, for She would make the final determination as to whether they would be made welcome. His prayer for acceptance of his people was made to the Land, the entity named Ériu. This is a critically important understanding, even to the degree that adequate production of food crops was one of the criteria upon which the worthiness of a king was judged. An inferior harvest was regarded as an indication that the Land may not have considered the king worthy to be her consort. Sovereignty is a critical concept in this process. It refers to the Divine right to rule and make decisions that is imparted to a king. The Goddess of the Land, is also the Goddess of Sovereignty. Sovereignty is of an eternal origin and is perpetual in that it doesn't expire with its holder; it is no one's property, it is a manifestation of the right of the Land to choose Her own king.

Water, in the form of springs, lakes, and rivers, is intimately linked to the fertility of the land. It also has a special importance as the vehicle in which offerings can be made to the local deities. Huge deposits of weapons, jewelry, and other goods have been found in Lake Neuchatel in Switzerland, Duchcov in Bohemia, the river Bann in Ireland, Llyn Cerrig Bach on Anglesey in Wales, and at the source of the Seine near Dijon in France. This is one of those practices that is still carried on today. Consider throwing a penny into a wishing well or fountain for good luck.

Springs had particular association with the Underworld because they bubble up from the depths of the earth; the water is either warm or very cold and contains dissolved salts that were believed to have healing properties.

Water also acts as a mediator between the other two realms, traveling from the sky as rain and returning as evaporating dew after making the land fertile. It connected humans with the Otherworld. According to Irish stories, at least some rivers were thought to originate in wells in the Otherworld and then flow into this world. Such rivers, wells, and springs were thought to carry the power and knowledge of the Otherworld to this one. The knowledge could be acquired by eating special salmon that lived in certain wells or rivers, by drinking from certain places, or by inhaling the bubbles that floated upon the river at certain times and places.

Fire is symbolic of the presence of deities and of the inspiration of poetry (*imbas*), it is also, like water, a vehicle for presenting offerings to the spirit realm. It has been recognized as a purifying force throughout the ancient world and the major Celtic holy days are referred to as fire festivals.

We recognize that trees and other plants are important sources of food, medicine, dye-stuffs, and building materials. They also connect us with the Land in a very basic and universal way because they are so freshly removed from Her bosom and still retain the undiluted effect of Her close presence. Trees provide an especially poignant revelation in regards to fertility of the land because they are deep-rooted and draw their nourishment from deep within the Land. They also act as a connecting point between our Middle World, the world below, and the world above.

Certain animals have specific metaphoric significance in the same way that certain trees or herbs possess a certain significance. Some animals are associated with specific deities who may have a propensity to manifest as that animal. Sometimes the animal is an expression and reminder of a particular virtue, strength, or ability.

Deer are often linked in the myths to fertility and the Otherworld, especially antlered stags who are often depicted with exaggerated antlers in early continental Celtic art. The growth and shedding of a deer's antlers mirror the annual cycle of the trees. Antlers begin to bud at the same time as leaves, they grow and flourish during the summer and are shed in the autumn, just like the leaves of the trees. Antler buds, like seeds, lie dormant during the winter months until the warmth of spring induces them to awaken. In Irish mythology Fionn mac Cumhail was closely linked to Otherworld deer—he could assume the shape of a human, hound, or deer as he saw fit and depending on the circumstances. He had a profound encounter with the Goddess of Sovereignty disguised as a deer, whom he had hunted and who transformed herself into a human for the occasion. They had a son, Oisín, whose name means "little deer."

The boar, because of its ferocity and fearlessness, was associated with war. Some Celtic warriors wore boar-helmets to battle in the belief they would terrify their opponents. They were also linked to the Underworld, perhaps because they were often responsible for the deaths of their hunters. In Celtic art boars are shown with enlarged ears and exaggerated spinal bristles, emphasizing their ferocity.

Dogs were often associated with hunting, protection, and healing. Fionn mac Cumhail's hunting hounds were his nephews in animal form. The Irish hero Cú Chulainn, originally called Setanta, was so named because he killed the hound of Culainn in self-defense and later offered to take the dog's place as protector of the homestead until Culainn could train a suitable replacement.

A healing water sanctuary dedicated to Nodens, a Celtic deity associated with healing, the sea, hunting, and dogs, was built on the banks of the river Severn in England during the third century, and all offerings to the God found to date are dog figurines. Anyone who has spent time around dogs would recognize that the expression "licking his wounds" originated in the observation that dogs do, indeed, lick their wounds clean to aid healing. Dogs often "nurse" injured animals of other species, including humans.

Horses are associated with fertility, sacred kingship, and the journey to and from the Otherworld. They are intimately tied to the life cycle of death and rebirth, the Land, and Sovereignty. The horse was a significant animal in ancient Celtic spiritual belief and an important animal in ancient culture. Manannán MacLir has a horse called "Splendid Mane," who is said to be swifter than the spring wind and can travel as easily over water as it does on land. The Daghda wears horse-hide boots with the hair on the outside and has a black horse named Ocean. Cú Chulainn had two horses that pulled his war chariot, the Black of *Sainglend* and the Grey of Macha, which were both foaled at the same time Cú Chulainn was born. Several figures from the Celtic pantheon could rightly be referred to as horse-goddesses— the Gaulish Goddess Epona, is perhaps the most well established with a wider distribution of references than any other Celtic God or Goddess. She is also the only Celtic Goddess known to have been honored in Rome, sometimes referred to as Regina. She is highly associated with the journey of the soul after death as well as with the welfare of horses and mules.

The Welsh Goddess Rhiannon also has a strong association with horses; she was said to be riding a "pure white horse of large size" when Pwyll first spied her. When her son, Pryderi, was stolen, she was accused of eating him and was condemned for seven years to sit by a horse-block outside the gates of the city where she would carry visitors into the palace upon her back, like a horse.

The Irish Goddess Macha is also highly associated with horses. Emain Macha (the twins of Macha), is named as the place where she gave birth to her twins; she died during the delivery after winning a race against the king's fastest horses.

Birds have held the fascination of humans forever, their ability to fly has been metaphorically related to freeing of the soul during death. Ornithomancy, the art of divination based on the flight patterns of birds, their song patterns, or deviations in their normal behavior, was practiced throughout the ancient world. Celtic mythology contains many instances of birds as Otherworld beings or as messengers from the Otherworld. Waterfowl were especially revered because they were associated with the three realms of air, land, and water. Geese, for example, are noted for their aggressive, alert nature and as guardians and protectors of the home, but they are also water birds and thereby link their protective function to the Otherworld. The crane is an especially important waterfowl in Celtic mythology, it is a supernatural creature who is depicted riding on the bags of human-headed horses and in connection with magic cauldrons. The imperturbable patience of the crane was associated with the Cailleach. On an ancient altar in France three cranes are depicted standing on the back of a bull. The crane is also a form of Pwyll, the Welsh King of the Underworld, and as such a herald of death.

There is a Celtic tradition that cranes are people transmogrified into bird-shape, possibly for a penance. Manannán's crane bag was formed from the skin of Aoife, Manannán's son's mistress, who had been changed into a crane because of her jealous behavior. This receptacle for the ancient Hallows of Ireland contained Manannán's house, shirt, knife, the belt, and smith's hook of Goibniu, the shears of the King of Alba, the helmet of the King of Lochlann, the belt of fish-skin, and the bones of Asal's pig, which the son of Tuirenn had been sent to fetch by Lugh. The treasures were only visible at high tide, at the ebb tide they would vanish. The bag was passed from Manannán to Lugh, then to Cumhal and finally to Fionn. The contents of the crane bag correspond to the Welsh Hallows of Annwn and to the treasures guarded by Twrch Trwyth.

Astronomy/astrology are crucially important concepts in understanding a Celtic orientation to the Universe. Imagine the great enlightenment that would have occurred when the ancients began to realize that the stars in the heavens moved at a predictable rate, and that certain phenomenon were related to the stars being in certain positions. Suddenly, people could anticipate when the rivers would flood, they could begin to piece together generations of chronological information regarding the migration of food animals and the harvesting of food crops. Naturally, this would have been seen as a great manifestation of the divine in this world; it was a predictable manifestation of the divine that allowed humans to be able to look into the mind of the creative force of the universe.

> . . . *they [druids] claim to know the size of the earth and*
> *cosmos, the movements of the heavens and stars . . .*
> PomPoNius MELA (c. 40 CE)

Some early Welsh manuscripts name constellations and even individual stars. The Sun, which provided light and warmth, had an unprecedented importance that was often reflected in Celtic art. Many ancient cultures, not just the Celts, adopted the symbols of the circle, spoked wheel, *triskele*, and swastika to depict the passage of the sun across the sky. Triskeles and solar wheels have been found on the remains of helmets, armor, and weapons of Celtic warriors, suggesting the patterns may have had protective symbolism. Some artifacts from Central Europe show the solar wheel linked to crescent shapes, presumably the moon. A sixth-century BCE sheet gold bowl from Zurich has depictions of deer, the Sun, and the Moon. The name Arianrhod, mother of Lleu in Welsh mythology, means "Silver Wheel," suggesting she may have been a Moon Goddess. Sirona, whose name means "Star," was a healing Goddess worshipped in continental Europe who is linked to the phrase "with light penetrating the darkness of night." The Gaulish Coligny Calendar is based on solar and lunar configurations.

Patterns of Observation

We have already established the positive role that living in close association with nature can play in establishing a healthy spiritual relationship with the physical world that surrounds us. Our ancestors had little choice but to work in accordance with nature in order to survive and could only have done this by close observation of natural phenomena. This observation might be analogous to our modern science of ecology. The term *ecology*, or *oekologie*, was coined by the German biologist Ernst Haeckel in 1866, when he defined it as "the comprehensive science of the relationship of the organism to the environment." In fact, a broader and potentially more descriptive term might be *systems ecology*. Systems ecology is an interdisciplinary field of ecology that takes a holistic approach to the study of ecological systems, especially ecosystems. It can be seen as an application of general systems theory to ecology. Central to the systems ecology approach is the idea that an ecosystem is a complex system exhibiting emergent properties. Systems ecology focuses on interactions and transactions within and between biological and ecological systems and is especially concerned with the way the functioning of ecosystems can be influenced by human interventions.

The importance of establishing these definitions in this context is to reiterate the fact that the interaction of many ancient and modern Indigenous people with their environments is/was a necessarily holistic process. The broader one's perspective and understanding of their environment and their relationship to it, the more successful one is apt to be in the short-term goals of appropriating food and shelter, and the more likely one is to take a proactive stance with long-term goals of ensuring survival under more inclement conditions. These are perspectives that have largely been lost to the modern Western individual; we have created a society that overemphasizes short-term goals and immediate gratification over more sane approaches to long-term societal health and viability. The ramifications of this modern perspective are evident in rampant pollution, global warming, overpopulation, and misuse of natural resources.

Here are a few observations that systems ecology leads us toward (with a little help from quantum mechanics):

1. Time and change are fundamental aspects of all experience (all compounded phenomena are impermanent).
2. Processes are ever-changing relationships with causes producing effects, which themselves are causes of further effects.
3. Causes and effects are defined as the coming together and dissolution of parts and wholes, structures and substructures, changes in relative disposition in space, energies, and attributes.
4. Physical substances can only be understood in terms of the disposition of their constituent particles and how these change and are changed by interaction with particles of other substances.
5. Relationships, dependencies, and interactions are ontologically more fundamental than "things in themselves," and "Process has priority over product."

6. Any "thing" that causes a change is thereby itself changed. Any "thing" that is observed is itself changed by the act of observation (not much use against a cannonball but effective against an electron).

The Celtic cosmological perspective sees the ultimate nature of reality in terms of three types of dependent relationships—firstly, by dependence upon causes and conditions; secondly, by dependence upon the relationship of the whole to its parts and attributes; thirdly, and most profoundly, phenomena depend upon mental imputation, attribution, or designation. All these relationships are constantly changing, and so all produced phenomena are impermanent and existence is merely impermanence viewed in slow motion, or so the theory goes.

These dependencies are described in many of the Celtic writings and might be able to be summed up in the Welsh conceptions of *gwyar* (change, causality), *calas* (structure), and *nwyfre* (consciousness). The triskele can be seen as a representation of the reality arising from these three dependences and has proven itself to be a useful meditative symbol. Celtic art, with its elaborate knotwork seems to be representative and supportive of an aesthetic and spiritual outlook of interacting and interpenetrating processes. The religious celebrations of many Celtic-oriented communities, including the Order of the White Oak and Tribe of the Oak, emphasize impermanence and the processes of becoming rather than the state of being. The changing seasons of the year are beautiful and tangible metaphors for the processes of growth, decline, death, and rebirth.

KENNETH PROEFROCK, NMD

Toward Your Own Ecology

Some Questions to Ponder from Ellen Evert Hopman and Kate Delvin, Ph.D.

Reflecting on Kenneth's words, here is an exercise that will be of profound value to Druids and others. The original queries were created by Kate Devlin, to which I, Ellen, added the more spiritual questions. Kate Devlin holds a Ph.D. in Biology from the University of New Brunswick. She has always had a deep love of the natural world and has wanted to thoroughly get to know each place she has lived, whether in farmland, a forest, or a small island. The following questions were adapted from an assignment given to Ecology and Natural History students at the community college where she currently teaches as an adjunct science faculty member. The original assignment had students choose a square meter of earth or a larger plot of land (not currently cultivated or part of a planned garden) to track over the course of a semester. Each week students were asked to spend some time in their spot, draw what they could see, and answer specific questions. As they learned more about the ecology of the area and its past and present history, they became more invested in noticing things. Many students grew attached and continued to follow their spots long after the course ended.

Druids and Groves can read and answer the inquiries in solitude or as a group. Druids could even create a book addressing these topics to pass down to their family and to future generations.

What is the history of your area? Which people(s) lived here before you? What do you know about them?

Do you know any of the ancient stories or practices connected to the land where you live?

What are the most important historical events that took place where you live, both in ancient and in modern times?

What has happened on the land? If forest, was it always forest? If cleared, was it always cleared? If wet, was it always wet? Was there once a farm there? How about an ancient village or settlement?

What was the land like before and after the last Ice Age?

What is the condition of the land now? Is it well cared for? Polluted? Built up? Returned to a natural state?

If the land is suffering, can you pinpoint the source of the problem?

What is located to the North, East, South, and West of you? Which important natural features or ancient sacred sites?

Which is the Sacred Mother River Goddess of your area (important to know so you can make offerings)?

Where is the source of the Sacred Mother River Goddess of your area? Where does she flow to the sea?

Which are the predominant fish, birds, and creatures that live in and near your Sacred Mother River Goddess?

Is your local Sacred Mother River Goddess clean or polluted? If she is polluted, do you know which industries are the source of the problem?

Where is the nearest source of clean natural water for you?

Are there any underground streams?

How far away is the ocean?

What plants grow nearby? Are these invasive species or native to the area? How many species can you identify?

Do you know nine edible plants in your area and how to cook and eat them?

Do you know nine medicinal herbs from your area and how to prepare them?

When is the best time to harvest these foods and medicines? How do you use them?

Do you cultivate any herbs, vegetables, or fruits? What grows well where you live, and which crops or plants have a hard time?

Do you know how to compost and are you composting your "garbage"?

Do you know how to maintain an organic garden?

Which fruits, vegetables, and grains are harvested where you live and when? Do you time your rituals to celebrate these crops when they are ripe?

Do you raise any animals? Are you aware of local farmers who are raising organic or grass-fed meat? How about free-range poultry and eggs? Do you buy from them?

Would you know what to eat from the wild in the event of a disaster?

Do you know how to make a shelter appropriate to the ecology where you live?

What is the elevation of the area where you live and how does that elevation affect the weather, plants, and animals?

Which animals live nearby? Have you spotted any tracks or scat? Have these animals always been there or are they newcomers? There is evidence that some species are changing their migration routes and habits with the change in climate, have you noticed this?

How about insects—have you noticed a change in the number or arrival and departure of certain insect species?

When you simply sit still in the field or forest—what do you hear? Smell? See? Have any new plants come into view? How about new animals?

What is the weather like? How does it change? Are there clear seasons? Are the seasons changing now that climate change is rampant?

Track the Moon over a year—where and when does it rise and set near your home?

Track the Sun over a year—where and when does it rise and set?

Have you calculated the Metonic cycle (eclipse cycle) yet?

Do you know which constellations rise and set with the seasons?

What is the soil composed of where you live? What does it look like? Is it sandy, clay, or gravel? Or is it dark and rich? Can you identify what type of soil it is? How does this particular type of soil affect the growing of plants in your area?

Does the ground freeze in the winter where you live?

Which months are winter months, summer months in your locality?

Does your area get a lot of sunlight? Or is it very shady? How many hours of sunlight does it get? Is this the same year-round or does it change?

How old is the oldest tree near you? Are all the trees around you the same age or are they different ages? How tall are they? What is their circumference? Are they healthy? Do they have a dormant stage or are they evergreen? Do any birds or other animals nest in the branches?

Is there a special tree, animal, or landscape feature that you consider to be your spiritual advisor? What kinds of offerings do you leave for it in exchange?

Druids and Trees

By Peter J. Quandt,
Associate in Applied Science Forestry
and Tribe of the Oak Druid

One of the things that distinguishes Druids from Witches and other Pagans is our unending reverence for trees. As I like to say, "Every tree is a church for a Druid." This is because in the presence of a tree, or even a tree branch, we are spiritually transported to the Three Worlds.

Trees delve into the Underworld of the Sidhe and the Ancestors via their roots. They dwell in the Middle World of the Sacred Land where the birds, animals, and humans abide. And they reach to the Sky Realm of the Goddesses and Gods as they stretch their branches to the sky. So long as a Druid is in the presence of a tree, maybe even one grown on the Moon or on Mars, we are in a place that is already sanctified and holy.

Druid Peter J. Quandt is a true man of the trees. He offers the following essay regarding his life's work.

ELLEN EVERT HOPMAN

The name Druid, by all accounts, is related to the Oak tree. Whether derived from the Greek *drus* or the Irish *daur*, the overall consensus is that the name is related to this species of tree. Add the Indo-European ending of *wid*, meaning "to know," and the name speaks of "One with the knowledge of the Oak," or "Wise person of the Oak."

With the northern area of Europe 80 percent covered in forest, it is small wonder that the Druids of that area were incredibly in tune with the natural world—and in particular the forest. At one time, most of the forest covering the territory of the northern Druids was of Oak trees, though a number of other species were available as well. Indeed, some of the "pioneer species" in open land turning to forest are the Juniper, Willow, Birch, and Hazel. Moving on further from the ice age, Ash and Oak, Elm, and Pine moved in.

The Druids viewed trees as living beings, with their own medicines, gifts, and wisdom. The first tree in the Ogham cipher is the Birch, which is also often the first tree to occupy open land, creating a grove that establishes a fertile place for other trees to take hold, which creates the forest. Its qualities are of renewal and femininity. The Yew, one of the longest living trees, is spiritually referenced with the powers of longevity and rebirth. Every tree has its own spiritual qualities, and when the Druid is focused and open, he/she can feel these qualities emanating from the trees. Douglass Fir bodes to "come sit with them awhile," an offering of meditation and spiritual connection. Alder emanates a sense of joy and brightness. Maple groves bring a magical quality of love that emanates from the ground up, as if wading in a shallow sea of it. Hemlock is nurturing, Cedar is shelter. Oak tree spirit qualities are that of strength, rulership, and power. Druids commonly held their rituals and celebrations in Oak groves. As a Druid visiting with the various species of Trees, I can always feel the quality of the wood of the Tree. I've been able to feel the density, the grain, and to some degree the texture.

Aside from the spiritual qualities that the Druids were aware of lie the physical qualities. Every tree species has some sort of fruit or seed to offer as food. Wood for structures, branches for fire, baskets, tools, and armaments. As well, bark and/or leaves from certain trees were used as fodder. The Druids did not separate the physical qualities of the Trees from the spiritual qualities. They saw the Trees, and Nature, as a whole, as single entities, yet connected to all of the plants, rock, earth, air, sun, water. The Druid takes the connection with the Tree to its total gifts in our world. As well, various healing remedies from the bark, flowers, and seeds made the connection with the trees of the ancient Druid world complete. Trees are symbols of physical and spiritual nourishment, transformation and liberation, sustenance, spiritual growth, union, and fertility.

The Druids based their spiritual practices on the cycles of Nature. They honored the flora and new growth with the coming of Spring. They basked in the celebration of warm Summer. They welcomed Autumn, as the prelude to Winter and the gathering of the woodland harvest. They understood the importance of Winter and the time to regroup and replenish for the coming year. Ovates were a class of Druids who made prophecies and studied Nature closely, with rituals linked to natural phenomena.

In British tradition the Oak King and the Holly King battled it out twice per year, on the events of the Summer and Winter Solstices. The Oak King is awakened at the Spring Equinox (Alban Eilir) and is at full strength at the Summer Solstice (Alban Hefin) defeating the Holly King. The Holly King is awakened at the Fall Equinox (Alban Elfed) and at full strength come Winter Solstice (Alban Arthan), regains his reign. Mistletoe was cut from the Holy Oak with a golden sickle and had to be caught before it hit the ground, usually with a white cloak or sheet. The Christian church banned cutting mistletoe on the sixth day of the moon to discourage practices that were not in keeping with the church's teachings.

Trees were seen as being connected to the three worlds:

The roots pierced underground realms of the Lower World, where Sidhe resided. The roots were thought of as doorways. Indeed, the root systems of trees are networks of interconnections, with a feel of standing among a vast communication system involving not only the individual tree or immediate community, but also deep into the other world. In dreams, roots represent our connection with our own human bodies.

Tree branches reach into the heavens, the Upper World. Breathing in carbon dioxide and breathing out oxygen, the leaves are the lungs of the trees, at the same time turning sunlight into energy. The branches mirror our own development, representing the directions and abilities we develop in our lives, the branch tips our aspirations, connecting to the sky.

The main tree stem (bole) lives in the Middle World. Here we can feel the vibration of the nutrients being passed up to the crown and water passing back down through, the way we direct our own energies of growth and development by thought and emotion.

Nestling in among the roots sitting above ground, or clinging to a hillside, it is easy to be aware of a communication system akin to our own telecommunications lines, though in a much more grounded and earthy energy feeling connected to all of the Earth. The branches carry that conversation from the Lower World into the heavens, emanating out and upward in a total connection with the Upper World, the stars, planets, and universe. The bole of the tree needs only to be aware, keeping in mind all of the seasons and weather, sensing the transfer of energy up and down.

In Ireland all clans possessed, within their own territories, their own Sacred Tree. Chieftains would have been inaugurated beneath the Sacred Tree, connecting them to the powers of below and above. Thus, the trees were seen as powerful and representative of the success of the king and his tribe. The Sacred Tree was seen as guardian of the province. The tree was said to have "sheltered thousands of men" (symbolically, not literally). To capture and destroy the Sacred Tree of an enemy was considered a very significant and demonstrative act.

In 981 CE the Bile (Sacred Tree) of Mach Adhair in Tulla, County Clare, under which the O'Brien chieftains were inaugurated, was torn down and destroyed by Mael Sechnaill, High King of Ireland.

In 1111 CE a County Atrim tribe cut down the Bile of the O'Neills, for which they later had to pay a compensation of 3000 cattle.[1] It should be noted that whenever such attacks took place, the trees were often replanted, or allowed to regrow.

In ancient legend there were five sacred trees considered the Guardians of the Five Provinces. These trees were said to have come to the court of the High King at Tara through an otherworldly stranger as tall as the trees themselves named Trefuilngid Tre-eochair. The seeds for the five trees were said to have come from the fruit of his branches and one was planted in each quarter of the land as well as in the center at Uisneach.

According the *Stair na hÉireann* (History of Ireland) blog, the five trees that grew from these seed were as follows:

Eó Mugna—Eó is the old Irish word for the yew tree, yet legend claims the Eó Mughna was actually a mighty Oak. It was said to have been a son of the original Tree of Knowledge, which some say resided in the Garden of Eden. Eó Mughna was the only one of the five reputed to have borne the three fruits, apples, acorns and hazelnuts, just like the branch from which the seeds were originally obtained. It was supposedly located at Bealach Mughna, on the plain of Magh Ailbhe, now known as Ballaghmoon, Co Kildare.

Bile Tortan—Said to be an Ash, the Tree of Tortu stood at Ard Breccan, near Navan, Co Meath.

Eó Ruis—The Yew of Rossa was said to have stood at Old Leighlin, Co Carlow.

Craebh Daithí—The Branching Tree of Daithe was also a great Ash, located at Farbill, Co Westmeath.

Craebh Uisnigh—This sacred tree, another Ash, was to be found at Uisneach, Co Westmeath a hill which stood at the heart of what was once the High King's territory, known as Mide. It was considered the very center point of Ireland, symbolized by the great Ail na

Mirean (Stone of Divisions), or the "navel stone", marking the point at which the country's provinces joined together.[2]

It is said that the five Guardian Trees fell together at some point within joint rule of brothers Diarmait and Blathmec, sons of Áed Sláine, who both died in 665 CE.

Brehon (judge) laws were the earliest laws. They were the laws of a pastoral people, whose economies were based on self-sufficiency. The agricultural economy was regulated by tribal and family relationships; wealth was measured in terms of cattle ownership.

Certain of the Brehon Laws dealt with Trees. Under these laws trees and shrubs were protected, because of their importance to the community. Penalties were imposed for any unlawful cutting or damage of trees, without the landowner's permission (branch cutting, barking, or base-cutting). Brehon Laws were also known as Senchus Mor or Gael Law. Dire (penalty) was a fine, in the form of livestock. Such as: 2½ Milk Cows for felling a "noble of the wood," 1 Milk Cow for a "commoner of the wood," and so forth.

There were four classes of trees, roughly mirroring classes in early Irish society, usually relating to its fruit, timber, or size, based on economic importance.

CLASSES OF TREES

Celtic Name	Translation	Trees Included
Airig Fedo	Nobles of the Wood	Oak, Hazel, Holly, Yew, Ash, Pine, and Apple
Aithig Fedo	Commoners of the Wood	Alder, Willow, Hawthorn, Rowan, Birch, Elm, and Cherry
Fodla Fedo	Lower Divisions of the Wood	Blackthorn, Elder, Spindle, Whitebeam, Arbutus, Aspen, and Juniper
Losa Fedo	Bushes of the Wood	Bracken, Bog Myrtle, Gorse, Bramble, Heather, Broom, and Gooseberry

As we know, the Druids had not only their gathering points in forest groves, but also had sites that they considered sacred, much the same as most any religion has (points of pilgrimage). These sacred sites often were in a place of special beauty, around a special tree, or a site of particularly strong energy that became gathering points for seasonal celebrations and events. Sacred trees and shrubs are also found in association with holy wells. As with other spiritual traditions, even the very route of pilgrimage had places of uplifting magic and mystical powers. These sacred routes were often associated with leylines. Michael Kelly, in *Wyrdwood: The Story of Dusty Miller*, goes into depth on the subject of leylines, the network of energy lines on the whole of the planet, which he says are "similar to the acupuncture meridians on the human body."[3]

The Druids were religious leaders, scientists, legal authorities, lore keepers, political advisors, poets, judges, theologians. They saw trees as powerful symbols of fertility, the abode of Goddesses and Gods, having their own God-spirit. Pliny, referred to the Druids as *Dryads*, whom he defined as "those who delight in the oaks." It is important to note that the Greeks called the tree spirits Dryads, whereas Pliny referred to the Druids as Dryads. Some believe that each and every tree has its own Dryad. Others consider the Dryad to govern a grove, or stand of an individual species.

There are conflicting beliefs on the longevity of Dryads as well. Some believe that the Dryads die with the passing of the tree. Others believe that the Dryad reincarnates through the seeds of the tree and therefore is immortal. Anything written about the Dryads speaks to the origin of the term from the Greek. Yet, the Druid was very much aware of the God-like spirits of the trees.

The deepest origins of tree folklore predate Christianity and is based on the beliefs of a world where all things were inhabited by Goddesses and Gods and spirits, and that core belief probably has changed very little for millennia. From the beginning of the Christian era, theology, science, and man have sought to explain away the "sacred" values of the various trees by taking into account their physical attributes.

With the onset of Christianity, many churches were built in Oak groves, and, in particular, near a large Tree. Opinions vary as to whether this was to draw attention away from the Druids and to the church, or if it had to do with the fact that lightning would more likely hit an Oak, than a church spire. It is a fact that lightning hitting the tree vs. the steeple is merely a characteristic of the tree (some say that it is just as likely to hit an Ash tree as an Oak), further evidence of its sacred status.

The deep-seated belief system of the Druids not only holds to the sacred qualities of the trees, but allows for both negative and positive attributes within the tree community. Some individual tree species were considered to be of a mostly negative spiritual quality. In observing the variety of trees, many of the negative qualities are offset by beneficial attributes. Trees that appeared to have a malevolent aspect, from a pre-Christian perspective, inevitably became linked to the story of the crucifixion in various ways. In observing the qualities of the variety of trees, it is clear that many of the negative qualities are offset by beneficial attributes.

The Druids knew of the value of Trees on all levels. Again, they did not know trees just for their physical gifts to the world. They knew of their spiritual, guiding, benevolent attributes. They knew them for their healing qualities on both a physical and spiritual level, as well as for their interconnectedness with all of Nature, including that which is not of this planet.

The Trees are the guardians. They are the largest of the plant life. Their roots not only tap into the Lower World, they are intertwined with the Middle World. The roots aid in holding soils, even mountains, in place. They communicate with all of life. The bole (stem) of the Tree provides for a constant flow of energy in the Middle World, as well as home to any number of animals from snake to eagle, panther to hummingbird. The bole serves to connect the Lower World with the heavens. The branches and leaves reach to the heavens, connecting with all that is above, honoring that, and bringing the blessings from the heavens down to this world.

The Druids were not tree huggers. They were the keepers of the knowledge of the Tree's connections to the three worlds. They honored and respected the importance of the Trees to our very existence, our ecosystem (both physical and spiritual). The Druids had the trust of their people, because the Druids had the respect for the Trees and all of nature. They knew how to respectfully use the wisdom placed in their trust, by the Trees. Everything about the connection with the Trees was with respect and honoring.

Visiting with the Forest, a grove of Trees, or a single tree entity is like going to church and standing among these beings it is as if one is in the greatest cathedral. One should not enter the domain of the Trees with our own agenda unbudgingly in place. For, in doing so, the greater blessings and wisdom could easily be missed.

A show of respect (perhaps a knowing bow or doffing of your hat) should always be shown, when entering the wood or standing before a great Tree. And, a thank-you upon leaving is more than appropriate. These manners will make the immediate connection so much the greater. The Druids know this, and we're always in reverence to the Trees.

PETER J. QUANDT grew up on the southern edge of the Adirondack Mountain Park. This beginning led him to attain an A.A.S. in forestry from Paul Smith's College and go on to spend multiple years working in a sawmill and cutting timber and almost four decades as a landscape contractor. In all of this time, he has felt a deep connection with Nature and especially the Trees. Working through the forces of Nature, many natural style landscapes, water features, rock formations and plantings have been channeled through his work. He has lived in Upstate New York, New England, Colorado, Oregon, and New Mexico.

He completed study in Mindful Outdoor Leadership at Kripalu, is certified in Reiki II, studied Druidism, completed a three-hundred-hour training in shamanic energy healing at the Four Winds, and is now looking forward to putting all of this and his relationship with the Trees together in a way that will best serve others, as he moves into the final trimester of this life.

Resources and Suggested Reading

These are the texts that Tribe of the Oak (**www.tribeoftheoak.org**) uses in its training program. They provide a firm foundation for a practicing Druid, including historical resources and literature, contemporary research and commentary, advice for the practice of Druidry, aids to creating rituals, and guides for celebrating the festivals.

Books by Ellen Evert Hopman

A Druid's Herbal for the Sacred Earth Year

A Druid's Herbal of Sacred Tree Medicine

A Legacy of Druids: Conversations with Druid Leaders from Britain, the USA, and Canada, Past and Present

The Sacred Herbs of Samhain: Plants to Communicate with Spirits of the Dead

The Sacred Herbs of Spring: Magical, Healing, and Edible Plants to Celebrate Beltaine

The Sacred Herbs of Yule and Christmas: Remedies, Recipes, Magic & Brews for the Winter Season

Scottish Herbs and Fairy Lore

Tree Medicine Tree Magic

A Trilogy of Druid Novels: *Priestess of the Forest, The Druid Isle, Priestess of the Fire Temple*

Other Useful Resources for the History and Practice of Druidry

Ancient Irish Tales by Tom Peete Cross and Clark Harris Slover

Beyond Celts, Germans, and Scythians: Archaeology and Identity in Iron Age Europe by Peter Wells

By Land, Sea, and Sky by Morgan Daimler

Carmina Gadelica by Alexander Carmichael

Cattle Lords and Clansmen by Nerys Patterson

Celtic Culture: A Historical Encyclopedia by John Koch

Celtic from the West, Vols. 1–3 by John T. Koch and Barry Cunliffe

The Celtic Gauls: Gods, Rites, and Sanctuaries by Jean Louis Brunaux

Celtic Heritage by Alwyn and Brinley Rees

The Celtic Heroic Age edited by John Koch and John Carey

Celtic Mythology by Proinsias McCana

Celtic Rituals: An Authentic Guide to Ancient Celtic Spirituality by Alexei Kondratiev

The Celtic World by Barry Cunliffe

The Celts by Nora Chadwick

The Celts by Otto Hermann Frey and Venceslas Kruta

Celts and the Classical World by David Rankin

Dance of Oak & Wren: Rites Of Draiocht by Robert Barton

Death, War, and Sacrifice by Bruce Lincoln

Early Irish Farming by Fergus Kelly

Earth Rites: Fertility Practices in Pre-Industrial Britain by Janet and Colin Bord

Exploring the World of the Celts by Simon James

Festival of Lughnasa by Máire MacNeill

The Gaelic Otherworld by John Gregorson Campbell

Gods and Heroes of the Ancient Celts by Marie-Louise Sjoestedt

A Guide to Early Irish Law by Fergus Kelly

The Historical Atlas of the Celtic World by John Haywood

Introduction to Early Irish Literature by Muireann Ní Bhrolcháin

Ireland's Immortals by Mark Williams

Lady with a Mead Cup: Ritual, Prophecy, and Lordship in the European Warband from La Tene to the Viking Age by Michael J. Enright

Pagan Celtic Britain by Anne Ross

Pagan Past and Christian Present by Kim McCone

Sacred Waters by Janet and Colin Bord

A Single Ray of the Sun: Religious Speculation in Early Ireland by John Carey

The Silver Bough volumes 1–4 (and any other works) by F. Marian MacNeill

Studies in Irish Mythology by Grigory Bondarenko

Understanding Celtic Religion: Revisiting the Pagan Past edited by Katja Ritari and Alexandra Bergholm

Where the Hawthorn Grows by Morgan Daimler

The World of the Druids by Miranda Green

Glossary

Archdruid: The chief Druid of a tribe, kingdom, or Druid order.

An Craobh Airgid: see *Silver Branch/Bough*.

Bard: an ancient Celtic poet who may or may not also have been a Druid. See also *Filidhe* and *Ollamh*.

bird augury: a system of divination with birds. See also *ornithomancy*.

Brehon Laws: ancient Irish tribal law.

corrguinecht: heron or crane posture or magical stance. A practice in which Druids would stand in the shape of a crane on one leg with one arm extended and one eye closed. The heron's, or crane's, stance was enacted to send out a potent satire or curse.

crane stance: See *corrguinecht*.

Cunning Man: the male counterpart of a Wise Woman—a man possessing folk knowledge of magic, herbs, and veterinary skill who worked with the commoners and was persecuted for witchcraft during the Christian dominance.

deiseal: sunwise, or clockwise (as in direction).

Divine Hag: a Crone Goddess, the Cailleach.

Druid: a highly trained practitioner of Druidism.

Druidism: the practice of ancient Celtic religion or a modern adaptation and interpretation of it.

Elementals: Spirits of Earth, Air, Fire, and Water, sometimes called gnomes, undines, sylphs, and salamanders.

equinox: days during which light and darkness are proportioned equally.

Filídh: the highest grade of ancient Celtic poet. They were the eventual successors of the Druids and practiced divination, magic, and law. See also *Bard* and *Ollamh*.

fire wheel: a ceremonial wheel that was lit and then rolled down a hill.

guiser: a person dressed in disguise for rituals. Also called a mummer.

handfast: an ancient Scottish tradition in which bride and groom pledge themselves to each other in a ceremony that precedes a formal, official wedding.

Hazels of Wisdom: sacred hazel trees associated with the Salmon of Wisdom (see page 162).

healing springs: mineral springs, such as the Roman Baths in Bath, England, typically dedicated to a Goddess or God.

imbas: poetic wisdom that descends suddenly from a divine source

Land Realm: See *Middle World*.

Lower World: See *Underworld*.

Middle World/Land Realm: the realm between the Upper World and Underworld. The Sacred Land where the birds, animals, and humans abide

Nature Spirits: the spirits connected with nature.

need-fire: a fire that is ritually built when there is a calamity (such as an infectious disease) affecting the entire community. See also Tein-eigin.

Nemed: meaning "sacred," the Celtic caste or class that included Druids and rulers.

neo-Pagan: the new, or contemporary, revival of Paganism.

oenachs: fairs, often during the Lughnasad festivals.

Ogham alphabet: the ancient Irish alphabet.

Ogham cipher: the Ogham alphabet inscribed on stone, vellum, or other surfaces

Ogham sticks (fews): sticks painted or carved with Ogham letters and used for divination.

Ollamh: a master of skill, an ancient Celtic teacher who had completed twelve years of school and had the modern equivalent of a doctorate. See also *Bard*.

omen: a sign interpreted as either auspicious or foreboding.

ornithomancy: a system of divination with birds. See also *bird augury*.

Pagan: A practitioner of an ancient religion, or contemporary version of it, other than an Abrahamic, monotheistic religion.

robur: Pedunculate Oak.

sacred smoke: smoke from a ceremonial fire. Such fires were used as fire altars and gifts to the Goddesses and Gods were deposited in them. The smoke carried the offerings to the Sky World of the deities.

sacred well: a well dedicated to a Goddess or God, often Brighid.

sacred wheel: a symbol associated with the God Taranis and also with the Sun and Moon in Celtic iconography. It implies the Chariot of the Gods as it courses the heavens.

Salmon Wisdom: a method of questioning meditation practiced by Druids that is an imitation of the observed behaviors of salmon, which they hold sacred. This is a term that came from my own imbas and which I explored deeply in my novels.

Sea Realm: See *Underworld*.

second sight: clairvoyance or precognition.

Seer/Seeing: the ability to "see" the location of lost animals and people and the state of their well-being. Also, a person with second sight (see above).

Sidhe: Fairy folk.

Sidhe mound: a mound in the landscape attributed to the Fairy folk.

Silver Branch/Silver Bough: a ritual wand made of wood with bells attached.

Sky Realm: See *Upper World*.

solar cross: an equal-armed cross, the Celtic version of the svastika.

sorcery: supernatural power acheived by the use of Spirits, the powers of nature, or divine assistance.

Summerland of Bliss: a pleasant land where the dead reside between incarnations. A place of endless feasting.

sunwise: clockwise direction.

tein-eigin: See *need-fire*.

Three Worlds: the realms of Land, Sea, and Sky. See also *Underworld, Middle World,* and *Upper World*.

Triple Goddess: a Goddess with three identifiable aspects. A High Goddess of the greatest power and skill.

Triple God: a God with three identifiable aspects. A High God of the greatest power and skill.

Tuatha Dé Danann: The tribe of the Goddess Danu, the People of Danu. A highly skilled supernatural race who ruled Ireland before the arrival of the Celtic Milesians.

Underworld/Lower World/Sea Realm: the lower realms where Sidhe and Ancestors reside.

Upper World/Sky Realm: the upper realm where the deities, the High Goddesses and Gods, reside.

Wise Woman: a woman possessing folk knowledge of midwifery, magic, herbs, and veterinary skills who worked with the commoners and was persecuted as a "Witch" during the Christian dominance.

Notes

What a Druid Is and Is Not

1. O'Duinn trans., *Forbhais Droma Damhghaire*.
2. Siculus, *The Historical Library of Diodorus the Sicilian*, V:31.

Historical Knowledge about the Druids

1. Caesar, *The Conquest of Gaul*, VI:13, 140.
2. Caesar, *The Conquest of Gaul*, VI:14, 140–1.
3. Kelly, *Guide to Early Irish Law*, 60–61.
4. *Annals of the Four Masters*, Corpus of Electronic Texts (website), 44–45.
5. Keating, *History of Ireland*, 130.
6. Fitzpatrick, "Druids," 305; and Crummy, "Stanway," xviii.
7. Siculus, *The Historical Library of Diodorus the Sicilian*, V:31.
8. Quoted in Bonwick, *Old Irish Religions*, 26–28.
9. Wikipedia (website), "Indus Valley Civilization: Language."
10. Macalister (trans.), *Lebor Gabála Erenn*, 110–13.
11. Zaehner, *Bhagavad-Gita*, 297.
12. Judge, *Bhagavad-Gita*, 73–76.

Goddesses and Gods of the Druids

1. Wilde, *Ancient Legends*, 242.

The Druidic Festivals and High Holy Days

1. Traditional verse quoted in McNeill, *Silver Bough*, 84.

2. Chadwick, *Celts*, 181.

3. Carmichael, *Carmina Gadelica*, vol. 1.

4. "The History of the Swastika," United States Holocaust Memorial Museum (website), August 7, 2017.

5. Pellegrino, "St. Brigid's Crosses and Girdles."

6. Carmichael, *Carmina Gadelica*, vol. 4.

7. MacNeill, *Festival of Lughnasa*.

8. Kondratiev, *Apple Branch*, 172.

9. Kondratiev, *Apple Branch*, 174.

10. Evans-Wentz, *Fairy Faith*, 80.

Druidic Wisdom Tales and Poetry

1. Quoted in Matthews and Matthews, *Encyclopedia of Celtic Wisdom*, 203–15.

2. Seán Ó Tuathail, "The Excellence of the Ancient World."

3. Seán Ó Tuathail, "The Excellence of the Ancient World."

4. Kelly, *Audacht Morainn*, 6–7, 17.

5. *The Instruction of King Mormac Mac Airt: Tecosca Cormaic*, Corpus of Electronic Texts (website), 45.

6. Richards (trans.), *Ashtavakra Gita*, 1.2–11.

The Tools of a Druid

1. Owen Jarus, "Possible Shaman's Snake Stick from 4,400 Years Ago Discovered in a Finnish Lake," Live Science (website), June 29, 2021.

2. Mary Jones, "Druid's Egg," *Jones' Celtic Encyclopedia*, Ancient Texts (website).

Druidic Meditation

1. Mayo Clinic Staff, "Meditation: A Simple, Fast Way to Reduce Stress," Mayo Clinic (website), April 29, 2022.

2. Erynn Rowan Laurie (trans.), "The Cauldron of Poesy," 1995/1998, retrieved from Kate & Corwen Ancient Music, Ancient Instruments (website).

3. Christopher D. Wallis, "The Real Story on the Chakras," Hareesh (Christopher D. Wallis's website) February 5, 2016.

Creating Druid Rituals

1. Carmichael, *Carmina Gadelica*, vol. 3, 301.
2. Carmichael, *Carmina Gadelica*, vol. 3, 287.
3. Carmichael, *Carmina Gadelica*, vol. 3, 311.
4. Doniger, *Rig Veda*, 189–90.
5. Poppers, *Little Love Book*, 76.

Charms for Divination and Augury

1. Adapted from Carmichael, *Carmina Gadelica*, (Lindisfarne Press), 170.
2. Carmichael, *Carmina Gadelica,* vol. 2,179.
3. Adapted from Carmichael, *Carmina Gadelica*, vol. 2, 181.
4. From *Lebor Ogaim* (The Book of Ogams), also known as the *Ogam Tract*, an Old Irish treatise on the ogham alphabet. It is preserved in R.I.A. MS 23 P 12 308–314 (1390 CE), T.C.D. H.3.18, 26.1–35.28 (1511 CE) and National Library of Ireland MS G53 1–22 (seventeenth century), and fragments in British Library Add. 4783.
5. "Ogham," Online Etymology Dictionary (website), updated August 19, 2019.
6. McManus, *Guide to Ogam*; and McManus, "Irish Letter-Names."

Charms for Abundance, Healing, and Protection

1. Carmichael, *Carmina Gadelica*, vol. 2, 153.
2. Carmichael, *Carmina Gadelica*, vol. 2, 139.
3. Carmichael, *Carmina Gadelica*, (Lindisfarne), 180.
4. Meyer (trans. and ed.), *Miscellanea Hibernica*, 19–21.
5. Carmicheal, *Carmina Gadelica*, vol. 1, 235.

Herbal Charms and Spells

1. Doniger, *Rig Veda*, 285–86.
2. Carmichael, *Carmina Gadelica*, vol. 2, 95.
3. Carmichael, *Carmina Gadelica*, vol. 2,103.
4. Carmichael, *Carmina Gadelica*, vol. 2, 109.
5. Carmichael, *Carmina Gadelica*, (Lindisfarne), 443–44.

6. "The Flower Clock," Gardena (website), Garden Life (section).

7. "Predicting the Weather with Plants," Almanac (website), September 16, 2021.

Druids and Trees

1. "Celtic Mythology: Five Sacred Guardian Trees of Ireland," *Stair na hÉireann|History of Ireland* (blog), December 1, 2020.

2. "Celtic Mythology: Five Sacred Guardian Trees of Ireland," *Stair na hÉireann|History of Ireland* (blog), December 1, 2020.

3. Michael Kelly, *Wyrdwood: The Story of Dusty Miller.* CreateSpace, 2011.

Bibliography

Aburrow, Yvonne. *Auguries and Omens: The Magical Lore of Birds.* Newbury, Berks, UK: Capall Bann, 1996.

Best, R.I. "Prognostications from the Raven and the Wren." *Eriu* 8 (1916): 120–26.

Bonwick, James. *Old Irish Religions.* London: S. Low, Marston, 1894.

Breatnach, Liam (trans. and ed.). *Uraicecht na Ríar: The Poetic Grades in Early Irish Law.* Dublin: Dublin Institute for Advanced Studies, 1987.

Caesar, Julius. *The Conquest of Gaul.* Translated by S. A. Handford (1951). Edited by Jane F. Gardner. London: Penguin Books, 1982.

Carey, John, "The Three Things Required of a Poet," Ériu 48 (1997): 41–58.

Carmichael, Alexander. *Carmina Gadelica: Hymns and Incantations*, New York: Lindisfarne Press, 1992.

———. *Carmina Gadelica: Hymns and Incantations, Volume I.* Internet Sacred Text Archive (website), 1900.

———. *Carmina Gadelica: Hymns and Incantations, Volume II.* Edinburgh: Oliver and Boyd, 1928.

———. *Carmina Gadelica: Hymns and Incantations, Volume III.* Edinburgh: Oliver and Boyd, 1940.

———. *Carmina Gadelica: Hymns and Incantations, Volume IV.* Internet Sacred Text Archive (website), January 8, 2018.

Chadwick, Nora, *The Celts.* London: Penguin Books, 1970.

Crummy, Philip, Stephen Benfield, Nina Crummy, Valery Rigby, and Donald Shimmin. "Stanway: An Élite Burial Site at Camulodunum." *Britannia Monograph Series*, no. 24: 2007.

Doniger, Wendy (trans.). *The Rig Veda*. New York: Penguin Books, 1981.

Dowling Daley, Mary. *Irish Laws*. Belfast: The Appletree Press, 1989.

Evans-Wentz, W. Y. *The Fairy Faith in Celtic Countries*. New York: Citadel Press, 1990. (Originally published in 1911 by Henry Frowde, London.)

Fitzpatrick, Andrew P. "Druids: Towards an Archaeology" in *Communities and Connections: Essays in Honour of Barry Cunliffe*, edited by Chris Gosden, Helena Hamerow, Philip De Jersey, and Gary Lock. 267–315. Oxford: Oxford University Press, 2007.

Gwynn, Edward (trans). *The Metrical Dindshenchas*. Corpus of Electronic Texts (website).

Hill, Penny. "The Healing Power of Dogs." *Friends' Newsletter and Magazine* (Friends National Museum Wales), September 2014: 17.

Judge, William Q. *The Bhagavad-Gita*. Los Angeles: The Theosophy Company, 1971.

Keating, Geoffrey (Seathrún Céitinn). *The History of Ireland*. Translated by Edward Comyn and Patrick S. Dinneen. Online: Ex-classics Project, 2009.

Kelly, Fergus, *Audacht Morainn*. Dublin: The Dublin Institute for Advanced Studies, 1976.

———. *A Guide to Early Irish Law*. Dublin: Dublin Institute for Advanced Studies, 1991.

———. *Early Irish Farming*. Dublin: Dublin Institute for Advanced Studies, 1997.

Kondratiev, Alexei. *The Apple Branch: A Path to Celtic Ritual*. Cork: Collins Press, 1998.

Macalister, R.A. Stewart (trans.), *Lebor Gabála Erenn (The Book of the Taking of Ireland), Part V*. Dublin: Educational Company of Ireland, Ltd., 1956.

MacCoitir, Niall. *Ireland's Trees: Myths, Legends, and Folklore*. Dublin: The Collins Press.

MacNeill, Máire. *The Festival of Lughnasa*. Dublin: Folklore of Ireland Council, 2008.

Markale, Jean. *The Druids, Celtic Priests of Nature*. Rochester, VT: Inner Traditions, 1999.

Matthews, Caitlin and John Matthews. *Encyclopedia of Celtic Wisdom.* Rockport, MA: Element Books Inc., 1994.

Matthews, John. *The Druid Source Book.* London: Blanford Press, 1996.

McManus, Damian. "Irish Letter-Names and Their Kennings." Ériu 39 (1988): 127–68.

———. *A Guide to Ogam.* Maynooth: An Sagart, 1991.

McNeill, F. Marian. *The Silver Bough*, Volume 1. Glasglow: William Maclellan, 1957.

Meyer, Kuno (trans. and ed.). *Miscellanea Hibernica.* Urbana, IL: University of Illinois, 1917.

O'Duinn, Sean (trans.). *Forbhais Droma Damhghaire (The Siege of Knocklong).* Irish American Book Co., 1993.

Ó Tuathail, Seán. "The Excellence of the Ancient World: Druid Rhetorics from Ancient Irish Tales." John Kellnhauser, 1993. Retrieved on Mythical Ireland (website).

Pedreño, Juan Carlos Olivares. "Celtic Gods of the Iberian Peninsula." *e-Keltoi: Journal of Interdisciplinary Celtic Studies* 6 (November, 11 2005), 607–49.

Pellegrino, Joe. "St. Brigid's Crosses and Girdles." Joe Pelligrino (website).

Pliny the Elder, *The Natural History of Pliny.* Translated by John Bostock and Henry T. Riley. London: Taylor and Francis, 1855.

Poppers, Elyse. *The Little Love Book: 267 Words for Love in Sanskrit*, 2nd ed. Los Angeles: LifeForm Projects, 2021.

Richards, John Henry (trans.). *The Ashtavakra Gita.* Realization (website), December 10, 1999. Updated August 24, 2023.

Ross, Anne. *Pagan Celtic Britain.* New York: Routledge and Kegan Paul, 1967.

Siculus, Diodorus. *The Historical Library of Diodorus the Sicilian,* book V. Translated by G. Booth (1814). Accessed online: Wikisource.

Wilde, Lady Jane Francesca Agnes. *Ancient Legends, Mystic Charms & Superstitions of Ireland.* London: Chatto & Windus, 1919. Accessed online: Project Gutenberg.

Zaehner, Robert Charles. *The Bhagavad-Gita.* New York: Oxford University Press, 1973.

Index

Page numbers in *italics* refer to illustrations and tables.

A special blessing on those who have read this book to the end!

Gods Bless each maiden and youth,
Each woman, man, and tender child,
Safeguard them beneath your shield of strength,
And guard them beneath the shadow of your power,
Guard them beneath the shadow of your power.
Encompass each goat, sheep, and lamb,
Each cow, and horse, and store,
Surround the rocks and herds,
And tend them in a kindly fold,
Tend them in a kindly fold.
May Lugh the many-skilled bless us,
May Danu's blessing flow to us,
May Brighid of the flocks protect us,
And our ancestors of the graves and tombs,
Our ancestors of the graves and tombs.
ADAPTED FROM THE *CARMINA GADELICA*,
"REAPING BLESSING"

———

níl deireadh ar bith leis an obair
(there is no end to the work)